scope of his concern: Men and Nature, Men and Machines, Men and Morality, Men and Learning, Ourselves and Others.

The Times of London wrote, ". . . if a test of a stimulating discourse is to provoke opposition, [these lectures] must be reckoned a considerable success"; and Alistair Cooke's advance review in the *Chicago Sun-Times Book Week* said, "Leach has suddenly come roaring up in England and no doubt will soon explode here, as the middle-aged hero of the rebel young."

Edmund Leach is Provost of King's College at Cambridge University.

Jacket design by Egon Lauterberg

D0860280

A Runaway World?

The BBC Reith Lectures 1967

A Runaway World?

Edmund Leach

New York
Oxford University Press
1968

Library of Congress Catalogue Card Number 68–24745

Printed in the United States of America

Contents

Introduction

As far as the author was concerned the theme of the Reith
Lectures for 1967 originated in conversations with Mr
George Camacho, Head of BBC Talks, and Mr Michael
Mason, who later acted as Producer of the series. The
central topic was to be the need for change in our moral
and social presuppositions in face of the galloping acceler-
ation of the population explosion and the technological
revolution, topics which have provided a favourite diet
for all the mass communication media for years past. My
subject matter was familiar enough though my evolution-
ist-humanist approach seems to have caused astonishment
and at times resentment. But here too the precedents have
a respectable antiquity. When the Ciba Foundation
opened its new conference room in Portland Place,
London, the inaugural proceedings took the form of a
symposium on the theme of 'Man and his Future' which
was attended by twenty-seven distinguished scientists of
international renown. The proceedings were later published[1] and in the concluding remarks the following
exchange is reported between Sir Peter Medawar, Sir
Julian Huxley and Lord Brain:

Medawar: I really do not know, even if we took a census

[1] Gordon Wolstenholme (Editor) *Man and his Future*. J. & A.
Churchill Ltd, London, 1963.

of opinion, what principles we would teach or what beliefs we would try to inculcate. This is the thing that has impressed me most about this meeting . . . the sheer diversity of opinions. . . . I think this diversity of opinion is both the cause and the justification of our being obliged to do good in minute particulars. It is the justification of what Karl Popper called 'piecemeal social engineering'. One thing we might all agree upon is that all heroic solutions to social problems are thoroughly undesirable and that we should proceed in society as we do in science. In science we do not leap from hilltop to hilltop, from triumph to triumph, or from discovery to discovery; we proceed by a process of *exploration* from which we sometimes learn to do better, and that is what we ought to do in social affairs.

Huxley: Much advance, both in biological evolution and in psychosocial evolution, including advance in science, is of course obtained by adding minute particulars, but at intervals something like crystallization from a supersaturated solution occurs, as when science arrives at an entirely new concept, which then unifies an enormous amount of factual data and ideas, as with Newton or Darwin. Major advances occur in a series of large steps, from one form of organization to another.

In our psychosocial evolution I believe we are now in a position to make a new major advance for instance in education. We can now educate people in the evolutionary concept and the ecological concept, neither of which were in existence a hundred years ago (except in a very rudimentary form) but which are now turning out to be very important ways of organizing our thinking about life and its environment. Indeed there are many important new concepts which we could bring out in a radically reorganized educational system.

Brain: We might end our symposium with a remark of Blake's: 'Without contraries is no progression'.

In the very first draft of my first lecture I included much of the above passage and though nothing of this, except an odd phrase or two, has survived into my final text it can now serve very well to indicate the *leitmotif* of all I have to say.

E.R.L.

13 January 1968   Cambridge

A Runaway World?

1 Men and Nature

Men have become like gods. Isn't it about time that we understood our divinity? Science offers us total mastery over our environment and over our destiny, yet instead of rejoicing we feel deeply afraid. Why should this be? How might these fears be resolved?

In the last analysis fear is always fear of the unknown, the threat of confusion. But this threat has many faces which alter as we change our talk. At one level, in public affairs, we call it 'the problem of law and order'; at another we see it as 'class struggle' or 'racial violence' or 'the ill discipline of youth'; but deeper still, in our private feelings, we worry about attitudes—the problems which are conjured up by words like 'detachment', 'objectivity', 'alienation'. All these expressions share a common element, a seedbed of fear: that common element is separation.

It is all part of a game which we were taught as children, the trick of language which takes people apart and puts them in their proper places. By using names we can put each of the countless things in the world into its proper box, separate, by itself. Living things are different from dead things, animals are different from plants, men from apes, adults from children, white men from black men, workers from bosses, myself from others. Words order our experience by keeping things apart. But this kind of order

I

quickly leads to a sense of helplessness: for what am *I* but yet another single, lonely, isolated thing at the mercy of all the rest?

But if we were not human and helpless, we should be divine and omnipotent. What could we do then? Suppose you were a god, what kind of freedom would you then possess which is denied to you because you are a human being? Men are subject to destiny: gods are not. Gods can intervene and knowingly alter the course of history; men can only experience what happens. Things happen to us: we do not happen to things. But although gods have free-will, they are not detached. Gods are creators, but they are not separate from what they create. Gods are not subject to natural laws, they are the laws. They are immanent as well as transcendant.

What I am getting at is this. We are accustomed to thinking of our human position as that of a passive spectator. We look on with amazement at the ever more subtle complexities of nature which the triumphant scientists display before us. We are eager to dig deeper and deeper into these mysteries. Yet we remain apart, alienated, detached. The scientist sees himself as explorer, not as creator. He takes it for granted that we must accept the rules of nature as we find them. He refuses to act 'like a god'.

But this detachment is an evasion of responsibility. Nature has not been fixed once and for all; nature is evolving. Science can not only show us how things are now, and how they have come to be what they are, it allows us to determine what shall happen in the future. Even the wildest fancies of science fiction are not far removed from possibility. If we so chose we could participate in the processes of nature in a quite unprecedented way and fashion a world to suit our own convenience. Why then are we so reluctant? If we have so much power, why do we feel dominated by events? Why do so many of us talk as if the advancing sweep of technology were a natural catastrophe beyond all human control?

If you ask a professional scientist that question he will probably simply reinforce your alarm by insisting that genuine human control is quite impossible. The argument runs something like this: Belief in human free-will is an illusion. In almost every situation that you or I might possibly encounter, we should already be fully committed, by genetic endowment or by the habits of past experience, to act in a predictable way. And even if this were not so— even if you could genuinely 'decide for yourself' what to do next—the choice could never be fully rational, because the long-term results of what you do will always be vastly more complicated than you had ever supposed. That being so, the wise man must avoid all involvement in practical affairs; only by detachment can he hope to gain true understanding. That last sentence is a Buddhist precept, but it also summarizes the basic philosophy of our science-laden society: All true science must aim at objective truth, and that means that the human observer must never allow himself to get emotionally mixed up with his subject matter. His concern is to understand the universe, not to improve it. Detachment is obligatory. It would be wrong as well as foolish for any scientist to accept responsibility for the practical consequences of his investigations. It is not the scientists' fault that we are threatened by the bomb.

We have all heard something like that before. But somehow it does not seem quite right, not even to the scientists themselves. The catch in the argument is that the detached objectivity of science is largely make-believe. Scientists do not just discover the truth once and for all; their discoveries have consequences which alter the state of the world, and the truth is then no longer what it was. Whether he likes it or not, the observer is always bound to get mixed up with his subject matter. That being so, would it not be more sensible to adopt a rather more subjective attitude to the whole business?[1]

Why must the long-term consequences always be left in the lap of the gods when we are so near to being gods ourselves? We don't know everything, but certainly we know a great deal. Why can't we have a science in which someone or other is prepared to take a personal view of how things ought to be and then try to bring it about? And let me be clear: I mean science, not engineering. It is not a question of whether we can plan road systems and cities; of course we can. I am talking about something much more fundamental. Are we prepared to tamper with nature itself—consciously and systematically? Can we accept responsibility for changing the life span of individuals, for altering the genetic endowment of human beings, for restructuring the balance of competition between all living things? Are we prepared to *plan* such changes instead of just causing them to come about, at random and by mistake? We can't evade such questions for ever, though we shall need a great shift in all our political, religious and educational attitudes before we can arrive at sensible

[1] This is a question not an answer. The answer which is offered by the lectures as a whole is that the necessary objectivity of scientific research does not absolve the scientist from responsibility for the uses to which his discoveries are put.

answers. Meanwhile orthodox opinion leans entirely the other way. Official science is fully committed to the principle of muddling through and not looking beyond the tip of your nose. All past experience, it is said, teaches us to take only one step at a time. Science should only concern itself with problems which have an answer. It is quite respectable to conduct intensive research into ways by which the sex of children might be pre-determined, but it is not the scientists' business to speculate about how this discovery might affect the future of mankind.

The reasons for this 'leave-it-to-fate' attitude are very complicated. There is an element of safety first. No one wants to shove his neck out and then prove to be wrong. But part of the story is that scientists are inclined to look upon historical change as an evolutionary process and, in their eyes, evolution has now acquired the status of a theological principle.

A century ago, Darwin and his friends were thought to be dangerous atheists, but their heresy simply replaced a benevolent personal deity called God by a benevolent impersonal deity called Evolution. In their different ways Bishop Wilberforce and T. H. Huxley both believed in Fate. It is this *religious* attitude which still dominates all scientific thinking about future development. Darwin's ideas belonged to the same phase of 19th-century thought as *laissez-faire* economics—the doctrine that in free-for-all competition the best will always win out anyway. But if the natural processes of evolution must in any case lead to the survival of the fittest, why bother? Conscious intervention by clever men can only serve to make things rather worse. It is surely much better to stand aside and just watch what happens?

5

But anyway the real crux of the matter is that the ideals of objectivity and detachment provide an excuse for steering clear of politics. A generation ago the Russian plant breeder Lysenko imagined that he could mould the processes of evolution to meet the needs of the Soviet economy. He was unduly optimistic, but at least his theories were in accord with the principles of Marxist-Leninism. And precisely because he was not detached, Lysenko never had any doubt about the rightness of what he planned to do. By comparison a British botanist would be wholly at a loss. Suppose, for example, that by altering the climate we could make vast areas of the Sahara and of the Sub-Arctic available for the production of low-grade food crops, are we unhesitatingly certain that we should want to do such a thing? But fortunately that would be a political question, so the detached scientist does not have to worry!

Somewhere along the line, this kind of evasion has got to stop. The scientists can't always expect to opt out of the tough decisions. All of us need to understand that God, or Nature, or Chance, or Evolution, or the Course of History, or whatever you like to call it, cannot be trusted anymore. We simply must take charge of our own fate. We must somehow see to it that the decisions which have long-term consequences are taken by men who understand what they are doing and not by bewildered amateurs. And it could be so. Change need not always be something that happens to us; it could be something which we choose to bring about.

But do not let anyone underestimate the extreme moral difficulty that any such god-like attitude to scientific knowledge must entail. Consider, for example, that very topical problem: the world population explosion. It is nearly always discussed simply in terms of food resources and Dr Malthus, but the real issues are far more complex. At first sight the facts look fairly simple. All over the world populations are rising and towns are growing; the rate of change is very fast and still accelerating—the consequences for our children and grandchildren look bleak and hungry. The fact that previous demographic forecasts have always turned out to be wrong doesn't really help. The arithmetic errors only modify the time scale. There may have been brief periods in the fairly recent past when the total world population has declined, but these were very much the exception. However much you fiddle the figures, it is quite certain that the long-term trend has always been up and up. And it is also quite certain that if the human population goes on increasing continuously at anything like its present rate then social life as we now know it will quite rapidly cease to be possible.

Now, the fact that we are aware that this is what might happen and that we have the technical ability to prevent it happening, poses a moral problem of an unprecedented kind. We *could* act like gods. Should we do so? Suppose, for the sake of argument, that we did collectively decide to limit the world population, what criteria should apply? Most of England is much more densely populated than most of India, but India is just now engaged in a campaign to limit population growth while we offer tax incentives to encourage large families. Which of us is right? How could we decide? The circumstance that, in the future, social life as we now know it may be quite impossible is irrelevant. The human species is very versatile. Over a very long period it has been evolving new types of social organization which permit denser and denser aggregates of population; at each stage in this process the people concerned have very quickly adapted themselves to the idea that this new style of living is normal and comfortable. If you could go back about 12,000 years you would find that no part of the human race was living at a density of more than two or three to the square mile; today some members of identically the same species feel comfortable in skyscraper flats at densities of several thousand to the square mile. Where do we stop?

This is a value problem, not a food problem. If human beings were content to live on a diet of modified plankton, I suppose that it would be scientifically feasible to have ten or twenty times as many people living on the earth as there are now, but they would have to live their lives in an entirely different way under conditions which all of you would consider perfectly horrible. And yet, if that Brave New World actually came into being, its inhabitants would think that everything was perfectly normal. This strange form of existence would correspond to what they had been taught to expect. They would enjoy living that way. Have we then any moral right to interfere?

Well, what do we do about it? Do we just allow events to take their course and hope for the best? Or do we try to tamper with destiny? We could set a limit on the total human population; ought we to try to do so?

The wisdom of past experience says: 'No. What actually comes to pass will not be what you now expect; if you alter the course of evolution, you will only make matters worse.' Well, fair enough; we certainly should not imagine that we could ever fully control the future. Whatever we do, history will still be full of surprises. But does this really matter? Surely anything is better than just being left out in the cold—scared stiff of what is coming next?

By participating in history instead of standing by to watch we shall at least be able to enjoy the present. The cult of scientific detachment and the orderly fragmented way of living that goes with it, serve only to isolate the human individual from his environment and from his neighbours—they reduce him to a lonely, impotent and terrified observer of a runaway world. A more positive attitude to change will not mean that you will always feel secure, it will just give you a sense of purpose. You should read your Homer. Gods who manipulate the course of destiny are no more likely to achieve their private ambitions than are mere men who suffer the slings and arrows of outrageous fortune; but gods have much more fun!

All right then; let's pretend. If you were a god and you could alter nature, what difference would it make? How far would you have to change your whole style of thinking in order to get thoroughly mixed up with everything that is going on? In my later talks I shall keep on coming back to that question. How far is the barrier that seems to hold us apart from the changing world only a matter of language and attitude? Is it that we are afraid of nothingness—that is, of standing alone in empty space— or simply of nothing at all? Is all our panic just a by-product of false expectations?

One of our fundamental troubles is that we in the 1960s —particularly, I think, we British—take it for granted that there is something intrinsically virtuous and natural about law and order. It is this expectation of orderliness which generates our fear of anarchy and which thus, in a world of accelerating change, creates a panic feeling that things have got out of control. But if we are logical it would be order, not chaos, which would now fill us with alarm. An orderly world is a world governed by precedent and experience, nicely organized to cope with facts which we already know. That would be fine in conditions of technical stagnation, but in the context of a technological revolution orderliness is simply a marker of how far the members of society have got out of touch with what is really going on.

This all-pervasive reverence for law and order has a bearing on what I was saying earlier about the scientist's devotion to objectivity and detachment, and this in turn affects the scientist's attitude to his fellow men. In the world of science different levels of esteem are accorded to different kinds of specialist. Mathematicians have always been eminently respectable, and so are those who deal with hard lifeless theories about what constitutes the physical world—the astronomers, the physicists, the theoretical chemists. But the more closely the scientist interests himself in matters which are of direct human relevance, the lower his social status. The real scum of the scientific world are the engineers and the sociologists, and the psychologists. Indeed, if a psychologist wants to rate as a scientist he must study rats, not human beings. In zoology the same rules apply. It is much more respectable to dissect muscle tissues in a laboratory than to observe the behaviour of a living animal in its natural habitat. If you inquire from the scientists themselves as to why they have these valuations you will find that it is the regularity and order of the physical sciences which are admired. The biological sciences come to be respected precisely in the degree to which they can make exact predictions. Conversely, the social sciences and the practical men are condemned because they are imprecise and because they are 'not sufficiently detached'. The underlying psychology here is complicated. The scientists are engaged in exploring a changing universe but they are frightened, just like the rest of us, by the idea of a changing society. So they try to keep scientific activity and social activity apart and pour contempt on those who get them muddled up. Good science is 'pure' science, and must on no account be contaminated with real life.

At another level the craving for certainty and detachment is a survival from the religious dogmas of earlier centuries which affirmed that the order of nature had been fixed once and for all by a single act of divine creation which had ordained, from the start, that the human species should be uniquely different.

Man, who was fashioned in God's image, has reason and free-will; all the rest is mechanical. The human observer stands apart; he is not personally involved. But this, of course, is just a fiction: in reality, the human observer and the stuff he observes share the same natural qualities, and this gives the whole business an uncomfortable air of relativity. The scientific study of nature is like Alice in Wonderland's game of croquet in which the mallets were flamingoes and the hoops kept walking off the ground. In this context, the scientist's insistence on detachment is simply an attempt to impose order on an unstable situation, a device to overcome the anxiety which arises from his inability to bring everything under human control. It is the modern substitute for prayer and primitive magic.

That needs elaboration. Until the advent of modern science, man had always expressed his feelings of incapacity in the language of religion. Human destiny was said to be governed by luck or fate or the will of God, and the ways of God were inscrutable. Man, by himself, was impotent. Yet this sense of human impotence was always qualified by a conviction that human affairs and natural events are so intertwined that the one can influence the other. Just as an eclipse might be taken as a sign of impending human disaster, so also the power of prayer and magic could provide the faithful with an assurance that, in the last resort, man is dominant over nature.

But in Europe since the 16th century that particular solution to the problem of human helplessness has become less and less acceptable. In times of drought the clergy may still pray for rain, but scientists pay more attention to cloud photographs relayed by satellite from outer space. Bit by bit the category of natural events has become separated off from that of human affairs; 'natural' is now felt to coincide with that which is orderly and certain, divine inscrutability now only applies to what is human. We are taught to believe that everything in the universe (except the human self) is subject to natural laws and that although these laws are very complicated they are all open to discovery. All recent experience seems to support this doctrine, and there seems to be no limit to it. The more effort and money we devote to research, the more regularities we are able to discover. Yet the old anxieties remain. Precisely because the scientist now sees himself as a detached observer and not as a participant he feels frustrated by his inability to intervene. His isolation from nature has cut him off from God.

The modern concept of nature resembles the older concept of God in a number of ways—'an act of God', 'a law of nature', either will serve equally well as the ultimate explanation for why anything happens at all. But in one very important respect the two ideas are diametrically opposed. God's ways are unpredictable: Nature's ways, if we work hard enough, can be completely understood.

But understood by whom? However much I try to stand apart, I still know perfectly well that there is no part of me which is not itself a part of nature. That being so, how can I be sure that what I discover about the world 'out there' is not somehow predetermined, or at any rate delimited, by the mental apparatus with which I do the discovering?

That is the really basic background problem against which the world of orthodox science tries desperately to maintain some kind of distinction between the human observer and what he observes. One response is to reiterate and exaggerate the contrast between nature and culture. Man considered as a biological species has all along been recognized as a part of nature, and his physiological processes have been subjected to intense scientific investigation. But the human person, that is to say, man as a conscious moral creature surrounded by the artificial products of his own creativity, is somehow not a proper subject for scientific inquiry at all. So experimental psychologists must play their games with rats in mazes, not men in houses; in zoos the animals are on one side of the bars, the men on the other—the stress is on how different we are, not how alike. And the same applies to the scientists themselves. Natural scientist and social scientist are whole worlds apart. A study of the electrical properties of snail neurones is real science; a study of human conflict is not.

But in their own style the social scientists are equally afraid of moral commitment. They simply fit the proposition 'man in society is a part of nature' to the orthodox doctrine that 'everything in nature operates according to principles which are open to discovery'. They therefore discuss human behaviour as if it were objective and external to themselves. Economists study statistics not human beings. For the sociologist, men in houses *are* like rats in mazes. And again there is the evasion of responsibility; the glib doctrine that scientists are concerned with how things are, not with how they ought to be.

What it boils down to is this. If you accept the argument that the only problems worth tackling are those which you have some chance of solving, then you must always assume, from the start, that everything proceeds according to orderly processes of cause and effect and probability. This applies whether you are dealing with a static situation or with a changing situation. So the very first basic assumption for any scientist is that the stuff he is studying is incapable of thinking for itself. It is not open to nature, or any part of it, to change the rules in the middle of the game.

But that precisely is the difficulty. Man himself is a part of nature, and he *is* now capable of changing the rules. Human beings can now transmute one chemical into another, they can create artificial substances having the attributes of living tissues, they can alter the genetic inheritance of living cells. Such actions are appropriate to a god but quite inappropriate to nature—as the scientist ordinarily conceives it. It is not vanity to say that man has become like a god, it is essential to say it and also to understand what it means. Since, god-like, we can now alter nature, including that part of nature which is man himself, we can no longer console ourselves with the thought that a search for scientific knowledge is its own justification. It has ceased to be true that nature is governed by immutable laws external to ourselves. We ourselves have become responsible.

2 Men and Machines

The marvels of modern technology fill us with amazement but also with dread. All the time we are haunted with nagging anxiety. Isn't the gadgetry getting too clever? Moon rocketry is all very well, but *Dr Strangelove* was much too lifelike to be funny. If the computers take over, where do the human beings come in at all?

But the anxiety goes deeper than that: where do *I* come in at all? It was all right when the surgeons just fitted us up with artificial arms and legs, but now that there are people going around with plastic guts, battery controlled hearts, dead men's eyes and twin brother's kidneys, there begins to be a serious problem of self-identification. What is there left of me as a human being if all the different parts of my body can be treated like spare parts to be bought over the counter of a bicycle shop? Am I just a machine and nothing more?

But surely there is a muddle here. We love our machines. Machines are what we desire most in the world. A car, a telly, a fridge, a washing machine, the very latest thing in cookers—what would we do without them?

Technical wizardry is just what makes life worth living, it is the badge of civilization, the marker which separates off the educated man from the poor benighted

savage who lives in a grass hut and cooks his food over
an open fire. So what is there to be afraid of? Where's
the worry?

I think the worry is that all of us are haunted by three
very big ideas which somehow ought to fit together but
won't. The first is the idea of nature: the world as it is
'out there' before human beings start messing about and
turning forests into cities and broad valleys into airstrips.
But nature includes the whole animal kingdom, and we
are animals. It was on this account that some eighteenth-
century philosophers maintained that the original pri-
meval man must have been 'a noble savage', an ignorant
creature of nature, who was inspired by sensual poetry
long before he became a rational human being. It is this
uncontaminated nature which modern science is now
exploring with such great success.

The second big idea is the opposite to the first: civilization as opposed to nature—what the anthropologists refer
to as culture—everything about our environment or about
our behaviour that is due to human intervention or to
learning as distinct from instinct, our roads, our houses,
our tidy fields, our manners and customs, our laws, our
language, and above all our machines, the gadgets on
which modern civilized life depends.

And the third big idea, which ought to bridge the
other two, but somehow does not, is much the most
difficult: it is the idea of the conscious self, the I. Am
I a part of nature or a part of culture? Well, both,
but how?

The trouble here is that each of us feels capable of
'acting intentionally', that is to say, we think we have
free-will; we think we can make choices. But where does

choice fit into the total pattern—the grand combination of nature, culture, and the human self?

We met this same puzzle last week when I was talking about the predicament of scientific detachment. The scientific observer can never admit the possibility that the stuff he is looking at might be changing in an intentional way. For change of this sort would produce events which could not be predicted, either as the outcome of mechanical rules or as the outcome of probability, and all scientific investigation would then become futile. Nature *must* be orderly, and we have the same feeling about the man-made part of our environment. The machines are all right as long as they behave in a predictable way; what terrifies us is the idea that somewhere along the line they might start making choices on their own—they might start to think, they might begin to act like us. And that would mean that we are no different from machines.

But why do you feel humiliated by the idea that you might be a machine? Why are you so sure that our human consciousness makes us something different, separating us off both from nature and from our own creations?

This is really very important. If only we could come to feel that consciousness is not something which makes human beings different and sets them apart but something which connects us all together—both with each other and with everything else.

Part of the trouble is that we still take our cues from the first chapter of the Book of Genesis. We still think of man as a special separate creation in a world of separate things. If we were more evolutionist in our attitudes we might feel more connected up.

Well, how about evolution? Evolution is a theory of change; a theory about how things have come to be as they are. But remember what I was saying just now about intention. The interesting thing about evolutionary change is that it is unpredictable; evolution is not a simple mechanical process, nor is it a simple randomized change process; can we then say it is an intentional process? Well, let's look at the facts.

The first thing we need to understand is that in nature change of any sort is rather rare. The most important process in biology is the almost incredibly exact copying of what was there already. The natural world of living things is quite certainly very heavily committed to orderliness and stability.

It is only because of this accuracy of reproduction that different species of living things can perpetuate themselves at all, so you might argue that, from a biological point of view, change of any sort is dangerous error. On the other hand, without such errors, all variation would be impossible. In general, species of living things become differentiated by becoming adapted to use particular resources of particular environments. By a sequence of slight changes extending over many generations the form of the organism gradually develops into a uniquely efficient apparatus for the exploitation of selected elements in its geographical surroundings.

As long as the environmental conditions are completely stable this physical specialization will ensure that even very similar looking plants and animals living side by side in the same terrain will avoid cut-throat competition. Indeed, the more specialized the diet, the more certain is the food supply. But a high degree of specialization of this kind could lead to total disaster if the environment itself were to change. Although all creatures, including man, are adapted to live in special environments, some are a good deal more versatile than others. They are less fussy about diet and can accommodate themselves to a relatively wide range of situations without drastic physical modification.

When the environment changes the more versatile species are at a great advantage. What happens can easily be seen by looking at your own garden. Most of the plants which you admire developed originally in rather specialized environments in other countries and if you don't go to a lot of trouble to provide just what they need they will die out. But the weeds are adaptable—no matter what you do you can't get rid of them. In the wild, weeds and rare plants are found living side by side but as soon as change is introduced the weeds begin to flourish and the rare plants to disappear.

Now in relation to all other species, we human beings are the weeds. We are all the time generating changes in the environment but, like rats, we can accommodate to all sorts of different situations, so the changes are always advantageous to us and disadvantageous to nearly everything else. In the long run we and the rats may be the only survivors.

But the puzzle I want you to think about is this: Any weed-like or rat-like kind of versatility calls for at least a rudimentary capacity for making decisions. In a situation of random choice, some choices are encouraged by the environment and some are not and, in the outcome, the species 'learns from experience'. But isn't that pretty much what we mean by 'conscious intention?' In that case is free-will really a human peculiarity? Are we unique at all? Well we are if you insist that 'intention' has something mystical about it, but not if 'intention' is just a special kind of mechanical response.[1]

This is tricky country. The margin between 'mechanical response' and 'intentional behaviour' is in any case very narrow. I don't want to push this argument too far. I am not suggesting that a sprouting potato in a dark room searching for the light should be described as 'acting intentionally', nor am I trying to deny that man is an altogether exceptional kind of animal. In the matter of language, for example, man is 'in a class by himself'. Human speech is a message bearing and information storing device of quite a different kind from that possessed by any other animal. All the same, we human beings are much less unique than most of you think.

It is only quite recently that scientists have begun to observe the normal behaviours of wild animals with real care, and the results have been surprising. It has become apparent that the classical distinction between animal behaviour which is governed by inborn instinct and human behaviour which is governed by reason and learning must be abandoned. Animals too can learn and in some cases they can pass on what they learn to their neighbours and to the next generation. Indeed, in the long run, learned behaviour can even have consequences for physical evolution.

For example, our own flattened faces and tool-using hands could only have become advantageous to the species

[1] The notion of *intention* is quite commonly used in a functional sense, e.g. 'the human heart is intended to function as a pump'. This sort of usage has no metaphysical implications.

after our ape-like ancestors had already learned how to defend themselves with weapons.[1]

Animals then—or at any rate some animals and in some degree—can possess 'culture', that is to say they can possess a body of hereditary knowledge which is not transmitted genetically. The main point that I am trying to put across here is that many kinds of seemingly standardized animal behaviour are the result of habit rather than of instinct, but that since animal habits, like human customs, can be modified quite rapidly—in years rather than millennia—we must accept the fact that animals can make choices. In that case the usual distinction between evolution on the one hand and history on the other largely disappears.

You and I were brought up to believe that man is unique because he alone belongs to history. At school we learnt about history and evolution as quite different 'subjects'. Evolution was something that happens to particular animal species; it is extremely slow and it is studied by scientists. History was something which goes on all the time in human societies and is studied by historians. The argument was that evolution is opposed to history, as nature is opposed to culture, as science is opposed to art, as order is opposed to chaos, as instinct is opposed to free-will, as body is opposed to mind, as animal is opposed to human being.

But by making this radical distinction between what is animal and what is human we get ourselves badly tangled up. We too are animals. The totality of any animal is not just the biochemical thing but also its behaviour, the way

[1] This suggestion comes from Professor S. L. Washburn's Huxley Lecture 1967.

it connects up with its environment and the way it modifies that environment. A bird is not just a two-legged animal covered with feathers; it is a creature which flies, a creature which builds nests in a very specific way, a creature which communicates with others of its own kind by means of sound signals of a special sort. Likewise man is not just a naked ape, with a special shape of skull, he is a creature with a uniquely versatile technical facility for modifying his environment and communicating with other members of his species.

But, you say, man is different because he alone can exercise free-will and intention. Well maybe, but maybe not; the difference is only one of degree. A kind of choice exists right through the system. In any kind of species, genetic endowment does not determine behaviour; it sets limits. It specifies what an individual cannot do—in our case we cannot use our arms to fly and we cannot see out of the back of our heads—but within these limits the individual animal—whether human or non-human—can adapt to the environment in any way it 'chooses'. And that choice is a matter of social organization as well as of individual behaviour. At this level the pattern of relations is not predetermined by evolutionary adaptation.

Of course man is different, but he is not totally different. What we need to understand is not what man is like 'by himself' but what he is like in relation to all the rest. Where do we fit in?

After that digression about evolution let us get back to the relation between men and machines. There are two rather different points I want to make here. The first is that the way a human being functions, just as the way any other living creature functions, is mechanical through and through. We have not got a special little private manikin sitting inside our heads pulling the strings. The other is that we should think of man-made machines as related to ourselves in much the same way as a bird's nest is related to the bird. The second of these propositions is much the easier to swallow, so let's have a go at that.

Every species of bird has become adapted by evolution to live in a particular way in a particular habitat; the nest which it builds expresses this relation. The bird uses particular elements from the environment to make the nest. If you substitute a different environment in which those particular elements are missing, the bird may, or may not, be able to make a suitable substitution. If it does manage to cope then the innovation expresses a new relation with the new environment. So also with us. Human beings with their gadgets are all the time establishing new relations with their changing habitat, but, in the human case, it is the human beings themselves who cause the habitat to change.

But I am going too fast. I have dragged in the difficult idea of 'relation' without explaining what I mean. I must make another digression. Let me go back to something I said in my previous lecture. When we first go to school we learn about the world by classifying things—kinds of plants, kinds of birds, kinds of insects. We are taught to separate one object from another and to label each item with its proper name. But later, when we go on to secondary school or to university, we gradually come to be far more interested in how things are related than in what they are called. This is because the comparison of relations is more thought-provoking than the comparison of things. For example, there is not much point in comparing a whale as an object with an airliner as an object; but you can easily see that the shape of a whale—that is, the set of relations which determines its outward appearance—and the shape of the fuselage of a large aircraft are very similar, and, as most of you will know, the reason for this is that the relation between a whale and the water through which it swims is very similar to the relation between an aircraft and the air through which it flies. There is nothing new in this: the whole point of mathematics even in its most elementary form—such as the formula $2+2=4$—is that relations have a sort of reality which is distinct from, and more general than, that of the objects which are related. Let's take another example. Supposing you wanted to answer the question: 'What is a motor car?', you could, if you liked, simply list several thousand individual parts by name. This would be description of a sort, but it wouldn't be much use. What most people want to know is how the thing works as a whole, and to explain that you would need to show just what connects up with what. You would almost certainly use mechanical models and diagrams and chemical equations without reference to any actual motor-car at all. In other words, the model—the 'network system of relations'—has much greater explanatory power than the thing in itself.

Almost the whole of modern science is like that; it is concerned with how things work rather than with what things are; it is concerned with relations, not with objects. But the habits of childhood persist. Although experience teaches us that relations are real and that things are to some extent a by-product of the way we use our language, nearly everyone finds it easier to think the other way round. Even professional scientists who operate in the mysterious world of particle physics, where all the experimental evidence is concerned with relations, and all the entities are entirely hypothetical, seem to feel that the existence of relations must imply the real existence of things which are related; so they feel obliged to invent names for things they can never see and even for entities like neutrinos, which, by definition, have no material existence! But that perhaps is by the way.

You see, the real point is this. We are all specialists of one kind or another—carpenters, bricklayers, cooks, electricians, farmers, doctors, philosophers, or what have you—and we all have our private languages. As the compartments of knowledge become more and more numerous and more and more complex, it becomes more and more difficult for the specialists to talk to one another, to swap ideas across the artificial frontiers of language which they themselves have set up. But when they do communicate, when a zoologist manages to say something to an aircraft designer, it is because we are able to make comparisons between 'relational structures' as distinct from 'material things'. And this isn't just a game for the boffins. It's what we all do, all the time.

Look here: I am communicating with you right now. I don't quite know what I am communicating, but I am communicating something. This is because the sound waves which are reaching your ears are organized in patterns which correspond to something that is going on in my head, and you are able to recognize the patterns: the patterns are 'relational structures'. They happen to be impinging on your ears in the form of air vibrations, but they are passing most of the way from this studio to your room in the form of electro-magnetic waves, and in my head, and in yours, the patterns probably take on some kind of electro-chemical form. But the patterning, the structure is the same all the time. It must be so, otherwise there would be no communication. But consider the communication path—my head, my voice, the microphone, the radio transmitter, your receiver, your loud-speaker, your ears, your brain. There is no break in the sequence. There is a transformation in the form of the pattern at each stage but not a change in structure.[1]

I think we can now begin to answer the question I posed right at the beginning: Why are you so upset by the idea that you might be a machine and nothing more? The trouble is in the way we use language. For most people the word 'machine' evokes the idea of a material object, made of metal, and full of revolving wheels and electrical circuits. If then I tell you that 'man is a machine' you immediately assume that I am saying that man is just one of Karel Capek's robots. But in my language the word 'machine' means something much more general; it is shorthand for 'a structured system which works'. From this relational viewpoint, any two machines which work in the same way or do the same kind of job are the same kind of machine even if they are made of quite different substances and operate in quite different environments. And we can usefully compare one machine with the other just as we can usefully compare the shape of an aircraft with the shape of a whale.

For example: Up to a point the human brain is the

---

[1] cf. Bertrand Russell, *Human Knowledge*, London, 1948, p. 272.

same kind of machine as a man-made computer.[1] Note my qualification 'up to a point'. I am not saying that human brains are the same as computers but only that they are relationally similar.

It is quite undeniable that some very useful analogies can be drawn between the relational systems of computer mechanisms and the relational systems of brain mechanisms. This comparison does not depend upon any close resemblance between the actual mechanical links which occur in brains and in computers, it depends on what these machines do. Brains and computers are both machines for processing information which is fed in from outside in accordance with a predetermined programme; furthermore, brains and computers can both be organized so as to solve problems and to communicate with other similar mechanisms, and the mode of communication is very similar in both cases, so much so that computers can now be designed to generate artificial human speech and even, by accident, to produce sequences of words which human beings recognize as poetry.

The implication of this is not that the machines are becoming so like human beings that they will shortly drive us out of business, but simply that there is no sharp break of continuity between what is human and what is mechanical. The machines are a part of ourselves just as our brains and arms are parts of ourselves, and the bird's nest is part of the bird.

Considered simply as a material object, a space vehicle, which can land on the moon and then carry out compli-

[1] cf. Medawar's valuable comment that even if it is inadequate to say that the human brain is a kind of computer it is certainly valid to say that a man-made computer is a kind of brain.

cated instructions issued to it from the earth and report back its observations in visual form, has an existence which is quite separate from that of its human makers, and it is pretty terrifying, but considered as a *machine* its status is wholly dependent; it is, in effect, an extension of the human beings who control it. It is as if man had suddenly been able to grow telescopic arms and eyes 240,000 miles long.

Up to a point this is comforting. If all man-made machines are simply an extension of man they cannot constitute a threat. But there is another angle to this. Those who object to the analogy between brains and computers are always telling us that 'computers can only do what they are designed to do'. Fair enough. But likewise human brains can only do what they are designed to do. This means that all communication between man and his environment or between one man and another man is subject to mechanical limitations.

The world 'out there' seems to be how it is because our human senses of sight and touch are part of a machine adapted to record just that sort of picture and no other. It is a fragmented world full of separate things ordered into sets on the basis of visual resemblance or similarity of texture. If we had different senses—more sensitive noses and ears, for example, or a capacity to respond to variations in the magnetic field—our environment would not only seem different, it would be different, even though the 'things' in it were just the same as they are now.

Sorry, that sounds rather mad. What I am saying is, that what the 'world out there' is like depends on how we react to it. It is relations which constitute my existence, just as it is relations which constitute your existence, and correspondingly what I can recognize about the world out there is sets of relations, not sets of real objects.

Let us put it the other way round. You and I both feel that we exist as individuals. If we reflect on the matter this must be because of a mechanical, somewhat computer-like process, which goes on in our heads. The brains in our heads are machines—products of evolution, adapted to record certain kinds of information in the human environment which are useful to man as an animal species; our brains cannot do anything else. What our brains record with the aid of our senses of sight, touch, hearing, smell etc., are patterns of relations, structures. The structures which the brain records must correspond to structures which are 'out there', outside our bodies. But that is the only thing we can possibly know about what is out there; that it is patterned in the same way as the responses in our brains. Therefore, patterns of relations are the only 'reality' with which we can have any real connection.

Things as objects are separate from us, relations occur in chains which connect up with us. Self-consciousness is awareness of relations; free-will is a matter of making adaptive choices between one possible pattern of relations and another. I am not a thing apart looking on; I am just the connectedness of one small piece of apparatus tied in with all the rest. A much more humble role—but less lonely.

3 Ourselves and Others

'Z Cars' and 'The Avengers' on tv, film posters, stories of sudden death, fables of Hiroshima: we are surrounded by themes of violence from the day we are born. It is not just nature and technology that seem out of control, it is ourselves.

If you measure violence by quantity then this is indeed an age of terror. Our weapons are more powerful than ever before; there are more people to kill and more get killed. But attitudes to violence change very little. War reports from Vietnam gloat over the horrors in much the same tone of voice as Icelandic sagas of the twelfth century; official communiques count the dead as if the generals were engaged in a grouse shoot—but this sort of thing has been typical of human beings ever since the beginning of history. Hitler tried to exterminate the Jews in gas-chambers; sixteenth-century Englishmen tried to exterminate witches and heretics by burning them at the stake.

In modern civilized states the insane may be subjected to brain surgery and electric shocks on the comfortable theory that it *might* do good, and that in any case the suffering victim could hardly be any worse off than he is already; by the same principle Vesalius and Leonardo da Vinci advanced the understanding of human anatomy by dissecting the bodies of condemned criminals while they were still alive.[1] When Stokely Carmichael urges his fellow negroes to kill their white oppressors he is only repeating Machiavelli's blunt advice: 'If you have an enemy, kill him'.

But why do we have enemies? Why should we seek to kill our fellow men? One thing you can be sure about, it isn't a matter of instinct. No species could ever have survived at all if it had an unmodified built-in drive to kill off all members of its own kind, because mating would then be impossible. The general pattern in the animal kingdom is that aggression is directed outwards, not inwards. Only in rare situations do animals behave like cannibals or murderers; predators kill members of other species, not their own. Fighting between animals of the same kind is usually a game—a sort of ritual exercise which allows one individual to dominate the other without either getting seriously hurt. There are human equivalents of this—duelling, boxing, playing football—but, in addition, we kill one another. How does this come about? My own guess is that our propensity to murder is a backhanded

[1] My critics have persuaded me that this accusation is unjustified. The criminals whom Vesalius dissected were fully dead; his limited experiments in vivisection were performed on dogs. For detailed evidence see C. D. O'Malley *Andreas Vesalius of Brussels 1514–1564*, Berkeley, 1964. My point would have been adequately met if I had reminded my listeners that throughout the 16th century, torture, lingering execution, and wanton cruelty, were considered to be a normal part of the judicial process. As late as 1607 an Archbishop of Canterbury sentenced one of his ministers 'to be fined £2000, pilloried, deprived of his ears, whipped until he confessed, and perpetually imprisoned'. His offence: 'libelling the episcopal government of the Church'—see Christopher Hill, *Society and Puritanism in Pre-Revolutionary England*, London (Mercury Books), 1966, p. 334.

consequence of our dependence on verbal communication; we use words in such a way that we come to think that men who behave in different ways are members of different species.

In the non-human world whole species function as a unity. Wolves do *not* kill each other because *all* wolves *behave* the same language. If one wolf attacks another wolf, the victim automatically responds with a gesture which compels the aggressor to stop. The gesture has the effect of an utterance. It is as if I attacked you and you cried out: 'Hi, you can't do that, I am one of your friends,' or even more submissively: 'I am one of your servants.' Among animals these responses are trigger actions. At a certain point the weaker party is bound to submit, and as soon as submission occurs the aggressor is bound to desist; so the victim of attack is seldom in serious danger.

The complication in our own case is that if a human victim is to be safe the attacker and the attacked must not only *behave* the same language, they must *speak* the same language and be familiar with the same code of cultural symbols. And even then each individual can make his own decision about what constitutes 'the same language'. I am talking to you in English, and you are listening, and you can understand what I say. This act of listening and understanding is an act of submission on your part. You are admitting that we are animals of the same kind and that I have the right to hold the stage. But this is a free choice. If you want to get rid of my momentary domination you don't even have to switch off the radio; all you need do is say to yourself 'I can't stand that fellow's fancy accent; he doesn't speak like me: he's not one of my kind.'

Let us look at this argument in a more general form.

Because of the way our language is organized and because of the way we are educated each of us is constantly finding himself in a position of contest. *I* identify myself with a collective *we* which is then contrasted with some *other*. What *we* are, or what the *other* is, will depend upon context. If *we* are Englishmen, then the *others* are Frenchmen, or Americans, or Germans. If *we* are the upholders of capitalist free enterprise, then the *others* are communists. If *we* are ordinary simple-minded citizens, then the *other* is a mysterious *they*, the government bureaucracy. In every case *we* attribute qualities to the *other* according to its relation to ourselves. If the *other* seems to be very remote it will be considered benign, and it then becomes endowed with the attributes of Heaven. China as imagined by 18th-century European aristocrats and South Sea noble savages as imagined by Rousseau were both remote benign *others* of this kind. Incidentally, modern technology has now so shrunk the world that this kind of remoteness has almost ceased to exist.

At the opposite extreme, the *other* may be very close at hand in direct relation with myself, as my master, or as my equal, or as my subordinate. In ordinary daily life we have to recognize dozens of these closely-paired, dependent relationships: Parent/child, employer/employee, doctor/patient, master/pupil, tradesman/customer, and so on. In all such cases the rules of the game are well-defined. Both parties know exactly how the *other* may be expected to behave and as long as these expectations are fulfilled, everything is disciplined, orderly and proper. But lying in between the remote heavenly *other* and the close predictable *other* there is a third category which arouses quite a different kind of emotion. This is the *other* which is close at hand but unreliable. If any thing in my immediate vicinity is out of my control, that thing becomes a source of fear. This is true of persons as well as objects. If Mr X is someone with whom I cannot communicate, then he is out of my control, and I begin to treat him as a wild animal rather than a fellow human being. He becomes a brute. His presence then generates anxiety, but his lack of humanity releases me from all moral restraint: the triggered responses which might deter me from violence against one of my own kind no longer apply.

There are hundreds of examples which illustrate this principle. In the 18th century, when reason first became exalted, madness became horrifying, and the crazy were herded into dungeons and caged like wild beasts. When British colonists first reached Tasmania they exterminated the local inhabitants as if they were vermin, claiming in justification that these original Tasmanians were not really human beings at all.[1] Hitler said much the same thing of the Jews. In contemporary South Africa apartheid rests on the theory that the blacks are members of an inferior species, and therefore incapable of understanding civilized law and order. Most of us profess to be shocked by such attitudes but our own behaviour is hardly any different. Criminals, lunatics and the senile are shut away from society because they have been declared abnormal, but once this abnormality has been established our violence becomes unrestrained. It is true that we don't go so far as to resort to extermination, but gaols and police station cells can be terrible places and, in many other kinds of closed institution, punishment and 'treatment' can barely be distinguished. Reprisal against the weak

[1] H. Ling Roth, *The Aborigines of Tasmania*, London, 1890, p. 171.

always gives deep satisfaction to the strong: momentarily, at least, it alleviates fear. Nearly everyone is horribly muddled about this. We persuade ourselves that punishment is a deterrent whereas mostly it is just vindictive.

We claim, of course, that our mental hospitals and our approved schools are intended to cure the sick and delinquent, but 'cure' in this context simply means compelling the unorthodox to conform to conventional notions of normality. Cure is the imposition of discipline by force; it is the maintenance of the values of the existing order against threats which arise from its own internal contradictions.

Notice at this point, how, in each generation, the special failures of society are shown up by the way that the orthodox manage to allocate blame. Before the last war many prosperous people talked as if economic slumps were caused by the unemployed who were said to be 'living in idleness off the dole'. Today our failure to create a world fit for young people to live in is marked by rabid hostility towards the young people themselves; they are held to blame for the situation which has produced them.

Just now with moralists and politicians, high court judges and Fleet Street journalists all teaming up together, the adolescent is having a pretty rough time. The youth of Britain, we are told, is hell-bent for self-destruction. What with pot and purple hearts, long hair and LSD, miniskirts and love-ins, student strikes and political demonstrations, along with a general confusion of rich sexy police court sensations of all kinds, the image of swinging Britain is one of total depravity. The young are talked about as if they were an anarchist fifth column. The old react with consternation. Should they exact summary vengeance or offer appeasement in the form of votes at eighteen? This is all very odd.

Tension between the generations is normal for any society; every son is a potential usurper of his father's throne; every parent feels under threat; but the present anxiety of British parents seems altogether out of proportion. Young people are being treated as an alien category—'wild beasts with whom we cannot communicate'. They are not just rebels but outright revolutionaries intent on the destruction of everything which the senior generation holds to be sacred.

Let us be clear about this. What is odd is not the behaviour of the young but the reaction of the old. By any objective criterion contemporary English society is quite exceptionally orderly. We are law-abiding to a degree which astounds most visitors from other countries. And we have been growing more conformist, not less. The classic evils of urban civilization—disease, drunkenness, prostitution—have all declined very sharply over the past half century, and nothing now causes greater public concern than plain evidence that the police are sometimes actively disliked. Admittedly the statistics show a numerical increase in the incidence of crime. But this is a measure of police efficiency, not of the moral state of the nation. Crimes are created by Parliament; it needs a policeman to make a criminal. You don't become a criminal by breaking the law, but by getting found out. You might remember that next time you get stopped on the road to take a breathalyzer test.

So what we have to consider is not 'why are the young so disorderly?' but 'why do the old imagine that the young are so disorderly?' and I hope you can see that this prob-

37

lem ties up with the topics which I have talked about earlier on.

It is because we feel ourselves separated from nature that natural phenomena such as the population explosion seem so alarming; it is because we try to insist that we are something other than very sophisticated machines that ordinary rudimentary machines become a source of fear. It is because the old allow themselves to feel separated from the young that the young create anxiety. What is it then about the present situation which should make the gap between old and young seem to be unusually wide?

Again, you must be on your guard against cliché explanations. Some people will tell you that youthful disorder is just a symptom of the breakdown of family life. I can see no justification for this. Nearly all the large-scale social changes which have been taking place over the past century have been of a kind that should have brought the children closer to their parents rather than the other way about. The shortening of hours of work, improvements in housing standards, paid holidays, the prohibition of child labour, the extension of formal day-school education, the disappearance of domestic servants—all these things should, on the face of it, have helped to intensify family cohesiveness. But in practice it seems to work out the other way; the adults are now inclined to treat the teenagers as alienated ruffians—and not wholly without cause. Teenage gang warfare and the systematic wrecking of public amenities is a reality. What has gone wrong?

Well, up to a point the old seem to be simply responding to visual signals. The young quite consciously go out of their way to look unconventional, and the old react by believing that the young really *are* unconventional. Quite a lot of the alarm is generated by sheep in wolves' clothing. But even if you should agree that the young are not really as rebellious as they look, you may still demand an explanation. What are the young people getting at? Why do they try to be so outrageous?

Well mostly of course they don't know, they are just imitating one another. But the leaders, who *do* know, have a perfectly good political case. They argue that they are the involuntary heirs to a generation of incompetents. Their seniors, who still keep all the power in their own hands, have made a total mess of things. It is these incompetent adults who manage the educational system and lay down rules about what young people are supposed to learn. The whole set-up is rigged to fit the belief that, when eventually the young grow up and come to power, they too will want to carry on running the show just as before. But this assumption makes co-operation impossible. If the old expect the young to participate in planning the future then they might at least take the trouble to find out what sort of future the young would actually like to have. Quite certainly the young do not want to inherit a social system in which power is the exclusive preserve of those who happen to have influential parents or of those who have shown themselves to be docile and obedient by conforming to parental expectations.

But the politically conscious are only a tiny minority, and the anarchist temper which prevails, with varying intensity, right through Britain's pop generation must reflect something far more fundamental. My own view is that it represents a really basic, and potentially very healthy, attack on English class values. Symbols acquire meaning because of their relation to other symbols. The 'aggressive disorder' of the young can only be understood in terms of its opposite 'orderly submission'.

19th-century boarding education for the sons of the English upper middle class created a new social category of great significance: 'The English public school boy', the prototype of unimaginative disciplined conformity. 20th-century day-school education for the children of the rest of society has likewise created a new social category 'the teenager', and the one is simply the inverse of the other.

In private, the two types do not really behave all that differently, though young people of today begin to adopt adult attitudes towards sex a good deal earlier than did their predecessors. But there is a sharp contrast in formal public behaviour. Where the typical public school boy used to be tidy, polite and respectful of established morality, the teenager sets out to be a kind of slovenly dandy, a blatant immoralist contemptuous of all convention. The point is that, in a very deep sense, the public school boy took for granted the values of an ossified, class-stratified society and was quite happy to continue the tradition by quietly moving into his appointed station; in an equally radical sense, his anti-type, the teenager, is in revolt against the whole principle of a predetermined social order. Even the fashions set by the mods three years ago are already completely out-of-date.

Social class is a very confusing concept. In a very general sense you can sort out the population of Britain into major social classes by using such crude distinctions as family background, economic status and occupation. But these are labels, not signals. Class as it affects our day-to-day behaviour is something much more intimate and on a much smaller scale. You do not recognize that someone is of your own class by looking at his weekly wage packet—you *know*. This is because any class conscious behaviour which you exhibit is always in response to a stimulus from outside. Human animals, when face to face, behave like any other sort of animal; they react to signals emitted by the other party.

But as I said earlier, our human case is special because of our dependence on spoken language and material culture. Any wolf can communicate with any other wolf by *behaving* in the right way; but a human being can only communicate comfortably with a very restricted number of other human beings—namely those who *speak* in the right way and use the right cultural symbols. In contemporary Britain the signals which trigger off the negative reactions which inhibit free communication are such things as accent, style of dress, the furnishing of a room, styles of food and drink and the hours at which they are consumed—in short, everything that might be covered by the ambiguous term 'manners'. Whatever is unfamiliar in any of these fields immediately marks off the person concerned as an alien stranger; someone with whom a relationship of friendly equality is impossible. If the gap in understanding is very wide we say that the alien is a foreigner; if the gap is narrower we compromise—yes, maybe he is British, but 'he's not our class'.

The old who operate this system seek to perpetuate it; the young inheritors seek to destroy it.

This links back to what I said a few minutes ago about people attributing youthful disorder to 'a breakdown of family life'. It is in the bosom of the family that we are first carefully taught to recognize and react to signals which indicate class difference, so any attack on social class will be felt as an attack on family values. Also many of the more futile and unpleasant forms of youthful protest —vandalism in churches and public parks for example— are intentional acts of sacrilege designed to shock the respectable family man. 'Oh dear, what are we coming to? Why can't parents instil a sense of public decency into their children?' And the criticism is fair comment, for family values have become increasingly focused on private status rather than public good.

It is not surprising that many of you should feel anxious but perhaps it is the family itself that needs to be changed rather than the parents. Psychologists, doctors, schoolmasters, and clergymen put over so much soppy propaganda about the virtue of a united family life that most of you probably have the idea that 'the family', in our English sense, is a universal institution, the very foundation of organized society. This isn't so. Human beings, at one time or another, have managed to invent all sorts of different styles of domestic living and we shall have to invent still more in the future. Technology and economics and family life are so mixed up together that change in any one always means change in both the others.

In contemporary Britain our ideas have been greatly affected by literacy and the use of the phrase 'The Holy Family' in religious contexts. Most people carry a stereotype in their minds which leads them to think that a 'typical' family consists of parents and young children, with mother at the centre, as housekeeper, and father, perhaps in a rather inferior status, as breadwinner.

Reality is much more varied. For one thing, domestic groups usually pass through a cycle of development lasting at least thirty years. The family starts out as a pair of adults; it increases in size, as children are born; then dwindles away again as children grow up and the parents die. The internal network of relations is changing all the time and it will differ as between one family and another according to the number, age and sex distribution of the children and the occupation of the parents. There is no standard pattern. But besides that, individual families are linked up with the outside world in many different ways. The external relations of a family can be based on any sort of shared interest—politics, sport, leisure time activities of all kinds—but as a rule much the strongest bonds are those of kinship, neighbourhood and common occupation. It is therefore of the utmost significance that today, in most parts of the country, the householders in any one street will not all be doing the same kind of job and will not all be related as kin.

This discrepancy reflects a very great change in our society which has come about mainly as a result of economic developments over the past fifty years. Up until the First World War a major part of the working population, both in the towns and in the countryside, was residentially immobile.

The variety of possible occupations open to working class people was small, and although there was a steady drift from the villages to the towns, most people had nothing much to gain by moving around from one town to another. In Lancashire, for example, practically everyone worked in the cotton mills, and there was no point in moving from Rochdale to Oldham or from Oldham to Bury. But today the go-ahead young man moves to the place where he thinks he can earn most, quickest, or he may even get shunted around from place to place by his employers. This change has had radical consequences for the basic structure of society. In the old days, bonds of neighbourhood, kinship and occupation tended to co-incide; most people spent their whole lives close to the place where they were born, so they were always surrounded by kinsfolk, not just brothers and sisters, but uncles and aunts, cousins, nephews and nieces, grandparents. Moreover, the girl whom a man married was often a near neighbour, and the two families were quite likely to be related already even before the marriage. It is still possible to find places where this state of affairs persists, South Wales mining communities for example, but the general pattern is fast disappearing.

The effect of this change is as much psychological as social. In the past, kinsfolk and neighbours gave the individual continuous moral support throughout his life. Today the domestic household is isolated. The family looks inward upon itself; there is an intensification of emotional stress between husband and wife, and parents and children. The strain is greater than most of us can bear. Far from being the basis of the good society, the family, with its narrow privacy and tawdry secrets, is the source of all our discontents.[1]

[1] I have been astonished by the public animosity provoked by this very ordinary remark. The contemporary English monogamous neo-local nuclear family with its matrifocal emphasis is historically an unusual form of domestic grouping. Although it gives a relatively high status to the wife-mother it presupposes that woman's natural role is that of cook-housekeeper-nursemaid; as a domestic ideal it derives from the larger patriarchal domestic household of the English 17th century middle class which Abiezer Coppe (1649) had in mind when he wrote: 'Give over thy stinking family duties . . . for under them all there lies snapping, snarling, biting, besides covetousnesse, horrid hypocrisie, envy, malice, evill surmising' (Quoted in N. Cohn *The Pursuit of the Millennium*, London, 1957, p. 370).
I use the word *tawdry* in the sense implied by the following Oxford

We need a change of values here, but it is not at all obvious just what the change should be. History and ethnography provide very few examples of societies constructed around a loose assemblage of isolated groups of parents and children. The domestic units are usually much larger and usually based on kinship. But kin groups can only function effectively if most of the members are clustered together in one place and this requirement conflicts with one of the prime dogmas of capitalist free enterprise: the freedom to move around and sell your labour in the best market.

I don't pretend to know the answer: all I am really saying is that it seems very likely that a hundred years from now the general pattern of domestic life in Britain will be altogether different from what it is now, and we should not get too upset if symptoms of this change are already appearing. Our present society is emotionally very uncomfortable. The parents and children huddled together in their loneliness take too much out of each other. The parents fight; the children rebel. Children need to grow up in larger, more relaxed domestic groups centred on the community rather than on mother's kitchen; something like an Israeli kibbutz perhaps or a Chinese commune.[1]

English Dictionary quotation from the novel *Lady Audley* (1862): 'an aspect of genteel desolation and tawdry misery not easily to be paralleled in wretchedness'. What I had in mind was the competitive pressures which force us to live beyond our means. In economic terms 'all trouble originates in an inability to pay one's debts'.

[1] My words were carefully chosen. I did not say, as several of my critics seem to have supposed, that either the kibbutz or the Chinese commune has been proved to be a viable alternative to the monogamous neolocal nuclear family as the normal domestic grouping in a modern industrial economy.

Fitting such units into our style of industrial economy could never be easy. But the economy may change, and there are many other possibilities. The Japanese, for example, have a free enterprise system which is comparable to our own but they manage their domestic affairs entirely differently. For one thing, they expect industrial firms to exert a degree of paternalistic control over their employees which Europeans find quite extraordinary. We need not follow their example but we too might be different in some other way.

But change at this intimate level will certainly not come easily. It is significant that most of us are so deeply committed to being alone in a crowded world that we turn the whole problem back to front: we worry about privacy rather than loneliness. I can well understand that feeling. When anthropologists like myself try to adjust to living a less fragmented life in the context of primitive society, the first thing we always complain about is 'lack of privacy'. Western visitors to Eastern Europe often react in the same way. But it is we who need to change, not the others. Privacy is the source of fear and violence. The violence in the world comes about because we human beings are for ever creating artificial boundaries between men who are like us and men who are not like us. We classify men as if they were separate species and then we fear the other. I am isolated, lonely and afraid because my neighbour is my enemy. But the young have seen through our absurdities and for the present at least they are showing a refreshing determination not to be corrupted by our self-destructive scheme of values. They deserve encouragement, not reproach.

4 Men and Morality

Those who dread the future are said to be demoralized. But the connection between fear and morality is complicated. A British clergyman, a Canon of Southwark Cathedral, told us the other day that 'Britain is dying for lack of cause, poverty of spirit, inferior work, inferior lives, and inferior ideas.'[1] That is certainly a thoroughly demoralized kind of statement, but self-righteousness of this sort springs from an excess of morality, not the lack of it.

In all these talks so far I have been trying to show you how fear of the future is tied in with non-participation. The intellectual scientific attitude which is characteristic of our twentieth century sets us apart from what is going on. We behave as critics of the play, not as actors. I want now to consider how far this difficulty is simply a problem of morality.

There are two sides to this. First there is the fact that all moral rules are conservative. Whenever we adapt ourselves to a new situation we are always behaving abnormally—that is to say 'immorally'—compared with what we did before. So in a changing world moral rules make all our difficulties seem that much worse. But secondly there is the problem I began to raise in the first of these talks.

[1] In a sermon quoted in the national press some time during August 1967.

47

Science has given us quite unprecedented, almost god-like, powers to alter the state of the world; what sort of moral principles should guide our use of these powers? To take a single case: our ordinary morality says that we must kill our neighbour if the State orders us to do so—that is to say, as a soldier in war or as an executioner in the course of his duty—but in every other case we must try to save life. But what do we mean by that? Would a headless human trunk that was still breathing be alive? And if you think that is just a fanciful question—what about a body that has sustained irreparable brain damage but can still be kept functioning by the ingenuity of modern science? It isn't so easy.

But what do we mean by morality anyway? I don't want to get bogged down in complex definitions. Moral rules are those which distinguish between good and bad behaviour, and the first point I want to make is that these rules are variable. Morality is specified by culture; what you *ought* to do depends on who you are and where you are.

The rules are most explicit about what is bad; the good is then residual. Sometimes the law supports morality; for example, it is not only wrong to steal, it is also a crime. But very often morality has to stand on its own. For a good Christian, sexual intercourse is always immoral unless it takes place between husband and wife, but in England, provided the partners are old enough and of appropriate sex and not too closely related, the law is not interested. In general, then, the enforcement of morality must depend upon emotion rather than policemen. In childhood we are taught to do right by the threat that mother will withdraw her love if we do wrong, but as we get older, our anxiety about parental disapproval gets transformed into a generalized fear of supernatural disaster. Retribution is inevitable. If punishment does not catch up with the sinner in this life, it will meet him in the next.

The content of moral prohibitions varies wildly not only as between one society and another but even within the same society as between one social class and another or between one historical period and another. Breathing apart, it is difficult to think of any kind of human activity which has not, at one time or another, been considered wrong. The Jains of India say that it is a sin to kill mosquitoes; the Jews think it wrong to eat pork; In England it is indecent to describe the sexual act in one syllable instead of three. It is wrong to wear outdoor shoes in a mosque; in some Catholic churches it is wrong for a woman to bare her head.

The wrongness of such acts differs in intensity, but there is no fundamental difference in kind between local conventions of manners and fashion and those which bear the deeper stamp of morality and religious duty, and the common belief that our more deeply felt moral constraints are shared by all humanity is simply a delusion. I do not think that anyone has yet met with a society in which it is considered proper for a man to have sex relations with his own mother, but universal morality gets no further than that. That being so, we are bound to ask: what is it all for?

Since moral rules vary drastically from place to place and from time to time they cannot have any long-term adaptive advantage either for the human species as a whole, or for any incipient sub-species. So why do we feel that they are so important?

Well, let us consider: just what do moral attitudes do? Let me remind you of what I was saying two weeks ago. All our experiences and all our thinking are processes which take place inside our heads. We pick up signals from the outside world through our various senses and then we respond to these signals in a mechanical way which resembles in some respects the operations of a man-made computer. The sensory signals tell us how things can be distinguished, how they react on each other and on ourselves; we infer what things are by observing how they work, and how they are mutually arranged. This applies also to relations with our fellow human beings. We observe how our neighbours behave, what they wear, how they talk, how other people behave towards them, what names they are given, and from all this we infer what they are and hence how we should behave towards them. But since our brains are computer-like machines of a particular kind they can only digest this information in a particular way.

There is a great deal about this process which still seems very mysterious, but we can learn quite a lot by studying the structure of spoken languages and by experiments in visual perception. In some fields the receptor mechanisms of the brain are quite definitely digital and binary, that is to say, they can only give answers of the yes/no kind, with nothing in between. You can demonstrate this to yourself quite easily. Take a pencil and draw a picture of a hollow cube with the sides all equal; what you have actually drawn is just a pattern of lines on a flat surface, but if you have had a normal European education you will always recognize this pattern as just one of two things—a cube sticking out from the paper or a cube receding into the paper. You can flick from one interpretation to the other instantaneously, but you cannot stop in the middle at the 'reality'. Or take the words 'bat' and 'pat'. If you are a native born English speaker and have some Asians among your friends get them to pronounce these two words in as many ways as possible and listen very closely to the initial 'b'/'p'. In a strict phonetic sense the sequence of possible noises here is a continuum—there is no natural break. But if your ear has been trained only to recognize English you will always hear just the two quite distinct alternatives 'bat' and 'pat' with nothing in between.

The basic point is this. In order that my brain may interpret a signal that is fed into it through my eyes or ears it must first of all discriminate: it must decide whether a particular line is going inwards or outwards or whether a particular noise is 'b' or 'p'. It is only when these either/or choices have been made that the interpretation process can start working. But notice how this act of discrimination calls for repression. We choose to see or hear a particular signal as either x or y, but to do this we must refuse to recognize all 'in between' shapes and noises. The 'in between' shapes and noises strike us as 'wrong'. I shall come back to that presently—but bear it in mind. I am going to argue that when we say that a particular behaviour is 'wrong' in a moral sense, it is because it struck us in the first place as an 'in between' kind of behaviour. It introduces confusion into our clear cut categories and we try to get out of the difficulty either by putting it into a special box labelled 'bad things' or else by repressing it from our consciousness altogether.

Let me pursue this matter of repression a little further. Our eyes and ears are designed to recognize contrast, and they convey information because our brains can be programmed to decode these contrasts. A remarkable example of this is the way we can manage to decipher nearly illegible hand-writing. The eye must first of all distinguish the shape of the message material itself—to do this it must repress any consciousness of random background marks on the paper. Then the various squiggles of the message material are 'recognized' as forming sequences of separate letters and separate words. Just how we do this I don't know, but somehow or other, by distorting the actual patterns on the paper and suppressing our awareness of various bits we don't want to use, we can decide what the patterns are 'meant to be'. It is only when we have thus corrected our visual image that we can begin to extract a meaning by seeing how the patterns are arranged. It is the combination of rectified shapes on the paper which adds up to a message, not the actual shapes in isolation.[1]

But what on earth has all this got to do with morality? Well, what I am getting at is this: When we observe other people's behaviour we are faced with the same kind of interpretation problem as when we read a hand-written letter. Before we can decode the message we have to rectify the signals—we have to fit what we actually observe to a model of what we have been taught to expect. And moral attitudes help us to do this. My morality gives me a model of how things are 'meant to be'. What the other fellow is really doing may be quite chaotic—like a

[1] It is not my thesis that the human brain can only make binary discriminations but only that in a great many fields of experience we are very strongly predisposed to do so. The actual electro-chemical processes in the brain probably result in analog rather than digital discriminations.

scribble on a piece of paper—but, with the model to help me, I begin to see it as orderly and meaningful.

As long as we think we can recognize what the pattern is 'meant to be' most of us are quite willing to tolerate even quite wildly unorthodox behaviour in other people, but there always comes a point when the deviation gets too great. Then we become confused; we don't know what is going on. However, by reclassifying the deviant behaviour as 'wrong' or 'immoral', we can push it aside and even remove it from our consciousness altogether. In this way we restore our confidence in an orderly world.

One striking example of what I am saying is to be seen in Charles Dickens' portrayal of low life in mid-nineteenth century London. Dickens' descriptions read as if they were copies from real life until we notice that, in their sexual lives, all his characters accept the prudish conventions of Victorian orthodoxy. For a fallen woman, the rewards of sin are inescapable. Little Emily, rescued at last from suicide and a fate worse than death, has to be shipped off to Australia to escape the unforgiving reproaches of society![1]

Now the contemporary sociologist, Henry Mayhew, records that in the London of that period there were at least eighty thousand prostitutes and that 'the troops of elegantly dressed courtesans' parading up and down Regent Street and the Haymarket were a tourist attraction famous throughout Europe.[2] These gay ladies must have been quite familiar to most of Dickens' readers, but because

[1] *David Copperfield*, Macmillan Edition, 1920, pp. 680–681.
[2] Henry Mayhew's five-volume work, *London Labour and the London Poor*, reached its final form in 1864. It had originally appeared in weekly and monthly parts under various titles between 1851 and 1862. The first edition of *David Copperfield* was published in 1850.

they were classed as immoral they became socially quite invisible. In a documentary novel they were unmentionable.

History offers us the same sort of warning. Great reformers, who feel themselves to be motivated by the very highest ideals, may appear in retrospect as major criminals. This seems to be because the immediate consequences of a great man's actions may be so far removed from his avowed moral intentions that he and his followers can deny their existence altogether. The tortures of the Spanish Inquisition fall under this head as well as the endless massacres of countless religious wars. And we need to remember that even in our own day both Stalin and Hitler were looked upon as saints by millions of their fellow countrymen even in the midst of the holocaust. In the thirties, the Russian and German peoples simply 'refused to know' what was going on right under their noses.

I think that we can learn something from such examples of self-imposed ignorance. The question I am asking is, can the scientists and politicians who have acquired godlike power to alter our way of life be restrained by the application of moral principles? If so, what moral principles? And the sort of answer that seems to be coming up is this: 'Beware of moral principles. A zeal to do right leads to the segregation of saints from sinners, and the sinners will then be shut away out of sight and subjected to violence. Other creatures and other people besides ourselves have a right to exist, and we must somehow or other try to see where they fit in.' It is like that problem of the cube drawn on a flat piece of paper. So long as we allow our perception to be guided by morality we shall see evil where there is none, or shining virtue even when evil is staring us in the face, but what we find impossible is to see the facts as they really are.

But why can't we see the facts as they really are? What is this reality which seems to get out of focus as soon as we try to bring moral judgement to bear?

Well the trouble is that moral judgements are about social relations and relations have no material existence. We can only 'observe' social relations indirectly by interpreting other people's behaviour, and we can only do this if we first invent an artificial code which attaches social meaning to cultural facts. Thus we all take it for granted that holders of high office will wear special uniforms and be addressed by special titles, and that special noises, like drum beats and trumpet calls, and even special smells, like incense, will be used to indicate the approach of exalted persons and so on. But the interpretations which we put on such signals are arbitrary. We interpret the code in the way we have been taught; there is nothing intrinsic about it. A European widow wears black, a Chinese widow wears white.

Until we know the code, the 'facts as they really are' don't carry any message at all. But once we do know the code we can fit what we see, or hear, or smell, to our expectations. The signals which get us into an emotional muddle are always the border line cases in which the messages are inconsistent. Let us take an imaginary and improbable case: suppose that you were to attend the funeral of a close friend of yours who had been a devout and rather conventional member of the Church of England. You would have quite definite expectations and in the particular context of a funeral you would find it especially difficult to tolerate deviation. Certainly if you found that all the near relatives had turned up in beach clothes and that the daughter was playing a transistor radio, you would feel shocked and indignant. But there would be nothing wrong about the clothes and the music in themselves; they become wrong because they are out of place, they are inconsistent with what you expect.

Or consider another example which concerns morality in a more straightforward sense. The sexual act is right in the context of the marriage bed, it is wrong everywhere else. In particular, our incest rule makes it a heinous sin for a man to have sex relations with his own sister; this is clear cut and consistent: a sister cannot be a wife. But what about first cousins? In Britain marriage between first cousins is allowed by law and is quite common, but society is confused; cousin marriage is *like* incest. So it becomes a matter of immorality. Many people feel that cousin marriage is bad and should be discouraged. Legend affirms that the children of cousins will be deformed, imbecile and so on. Just in case you yourself believe in this mythology I had better point out that in most parts of the world marriage between first cousins is very strongly approved.

Let me repeat the main points I have been making here. When we evaluate other people's behaviour we do so according to a code which we have been taught. The code is arbitrary. It changes as we move across the map from one place to another, or through time from one generation to another. The code tends to be binary, that is to say, it offers at each stage of interpretation only two alternatives: yes/no; right/wrong. Generally speaking, we are able to make sense out of our observations by refusing to notice events which do not fit our expectations. But there is always a certain amount of marginal stuff which we are not sure about: is it right, or is it wrong? And this gets us worried. When social conditions are changing fast, this area of uncertainty gets larger. The old start to denounce the young for their immorality because the code is changing, and they can no longer interpret the signals. But it is still all a question of interpretation; there is no way of saying what the facts really are. In their own estimation the psychedelic hippies with their marijuana and their LSD are primitive Christians proclaiming the brotherhood of man; in the eyes of many of their seniors their activities are a close approximation to witchcraft and the Black Mass. Either might be right.

But let me go back to my earlier point: moral judgements are about social relations. In a formal sense a social relationship is the link between a pair of opposed roles. For example, if you take a series of paired terms such as father/son, husband/wife, doctor/patient, employer/employee, then morality specifies what is the 'correct' behaviour of each party towards the other.

There is always an element of exchange: each party has rights, each party has obligations, and the fulfilment of these mutual services is morally coercive. Whenever I accept any kind of gift, whether it is in the form of goods, or money, or services, or simply words, I feel myself under an obligation to respond—that is, to give something back in return. It is this moral network of obligations to repay indebtedness which constitutes the structure of society, and if we try to dislocate it we are likely to generate a great deal of emotional distress on all sides. But there is a converse to this. When I give gifts to other people I expect them to respond in predictable ways. The response need

57

not be exactly predictable, but it must be near enough to rate as 'correct'. As long as that condition is satisfied I shall feel that I am in control of the situation and that the receivers of my gifts are good people. But if the response is totally unexpected, then I am beset by fear and I shall interpret the situation as morally evil.

One consequence of this coercive feed-back is that we are led to put a conservative moral pressure on all those who provide social services.

Let me elaborate. If you call a man a scientist or a research worker you expect him to be enterprising. Scientists are expected to explore the unknown, make discoveries, create innovations, experiment—so long as you yourself are not part of the experiment. But if you call a man a doctor or a schoolmaster you immediately imply the existence of patients and pupils and you have strong moral feelings about how patients and pupils ought to be treated. Doctors and schoolmasters ought to be up-to-date—but they must not experiment—not with *my* family anyway. Nobody wants to be treated like a laboratory guinea pig.

So although it must be perfectly obvious that medical and educational knowledge could only advance if there were a great deal of straightforward experiment with human subjects, these facts are 'blacked out', like the Regent Street courtesans of 1850. Since the experiments contravene the orthodox canons of morality they somehow become socially invisible.

This is a serious matter. If there is a discrepancy between how we think human subjects ought to be treated— in schools, in hospitals, in laboratories, in prisons—and how they are actually treated, then there ought to be reasoned discussion of the possible consequences. But, in practice, many of the ethical problems which crop up in these areas are so hedged about with moral reticence that we never really tackle them at all—not out in the open. How often have you asked yourself straight out: Is it really the doctor's duty to save human life in all circumstances? Anyway, what does the question mean? When does a foetus become a human being? Is there a stage of abnormality, or of senility, or of chronic pain when the preservation of life would itself become immoral? The ethics of this problem are enormously complicated but they belong to that deeply tabooed area of immorality which most people reject from their consciousness altogether. Some of the facts that need to be considered are these: modern medicine has given the doctor almost unbelievable powers to preserve alive creatures that nature would previously have destroyed, power to change the life prospects of children still in the womb, to alter the personality of the living, and to extend the life span of the senile. But if these powers of preservation are exercised in uninhibited fashion while, at the same time, we try to tackle the population explosion by reducing the birth rate, then the outcome will be a very decrepit conservative society in which all the political and economic advantages will lie with the very old. Most people will dodder on until they are nearly a hundred and half the adult population will be well past retiring age. I don't believe that that sort of society would be tolerable to anybody. But what is the alternative? The trouble arises from our moral inconsistencies—we fail to follow through the logical connection between this and that. We can all see that unlimited population growth must ultimately lead to the disappearance of human society as we now know it and most people have come round to admitting that this gives ethical justification to the limitation of life through contraception or abortion, but the vast majority are still deeply shocked at the mere idea that a doctor should ever of his own initiative wilfully terminate the life of anyone who has already acquired a human personality by the fact of being born.

There are deep problems here which are of great consequence for all of us and it seems to me that the only way out is to have a long period of public discussion so that, in the end, we, or our successors, may come to put a different valuation on the preservation of life as an end in itself. At present, our moral reticence—our ability to 'refuse to notice' anything we think ought not to be there —makes it extraordinarily difficult to face up to such ethical revaluations. On the contrary, moral reticence supports the orthodox intellectual attitude of scientific detachment; it encourages us not to get ourselves contaminated with the beastly facts of practical reality.

I cannot offer you any solution but let me try to explain the kind of ethical revaluation which I have in mind. Let us go back to this question of the population explosion. What is the background?

All species of living things, including men, have been endowed with a capacity to reproduce themselves in enormous numbers but, ordinarily, this super-abundant fecundity is self balancing. Animals and plants and bacteria are inter-dependent; they supply each other with food, but they also interact so as to limit each other's population. But our human position has now become altogether exceptional. We have learnt how the 'balance of nature' works but, simultaneously, we have also learnt how to frustrate its operation, and because at this particu-

lar point in history the whole civilized world is dominated
by our ethnocentric Christian ethic which puts such stress
on the fostering of individual human life regardless of
circumstances, we are for ever tampering with nature in
such a way as to favour the increase of human populations
at the expense of everything else. In the end, the hungry
bitter end, human interference will be self correcting, but
it would surely be odd if in the meantime our Christian
morality should lead us to avoid having children so as to
have sufficient resources to preserve the lives of the
maimed, and the senile, and the half-witted?

It is hard to say such things, and I repeat: I myself have
no solution. But it seems to me that at some point we may
need a new religious attitude. In some forms of Hinduism
the three prime aspects of deity are thought of as the con-
sorts of God the Father. There is Parvati the Creator,
Durga the Preserver, and Kali the Destroyer, and the
greatest of these is Kali.[1] Our Christian ethic stresses only
creation and preservation, so we stand in fear of death.

Men have become like gods, but we must remember that
although gods create they also destroy: gods are the source
of good, but also the source of evil. We too must accept
our dual responsibility and come to terms with the fact
that the total elimination of disease would be an entirely
intolerable blessing.

[1] Like any other pocket version of complex theological ideas this
is a crude oversimplification. Just as Christians claim that they
reverence 'three persons but one god' so also the separate named
divinities of Hindu mythology are all aspects of a single divine principle. Certainly Kali ('Time') has other theological implications
besides death and destruction. See H. Zimmer, *Myths and Symbols in
Indian Art and Civilization*, New York (Harper Torchbooks), 1962,
pp. 210–216.

5 Men and Learning

I keep on coming back to the same paradox. We are afraid of confusion, but the avoidance of confusion generates fear. Ambiguity worries us because we like the world to be tidy—yes or no, white or black, good or bad. But if we do get things sorted out into these nice clear-cut oversimplified categories, we find ourselves taking sides, and this leads to violence.

There is nothing new about this. Everyone agrees that most public discussion oscillates wildly between total confusion and crude over-simplification. But the usual excuse is that this is just a symptom of ignorance. People often talk as if the solution were quite simple: we just need more and better education.

Let's think about this. What does education do? Does it really help to clear the fog of prejudice? Will 'better' education really make it any easier to cope with the consequences of our ever-expanding technology? Our ideas about education are themselves distorted by the process of classification. Education is 'what we do at school', it is a matter of acquiring knowledge, and knowledge is broken up into a variety of 'subjects'; mathematics, geography, history, French and so on. This 'what we do at school' gets contrasted with 'what we do at home'. So the word 'education' suggests school life not home life. Then again schoolteachers are for ever telling their pupils to work hard at their lessons and not play about, otherwise they will be punished, but later, after we leave school, work comes to mean what we do in the factory or the office, while play is what we do in our free time, and this reinforces our earlier ideas. In effect we are taught that education is an unpleasant process to which we are forced to submit when we are away from home. So although education is a 'good thing' it is always felt to be work, a kind of necessary evil; it is part of the rat race whereby we get on in the world and earn more money, not something that is a delight in itself.

Of course, I realize that many of you who are listening to me, use the word 'education' in a much broader sense, but you must admit that in common speech it means the drudgery of schooling and not much else. Anyway, for the next few minutes I should like you to put this convention quite on one side. The education I want to talk about is the total process whereby newly born speechless infants are reared and taught to play their roles as adult human beings. This kind of education begins at birth and ends at death; we learn much faster at the age of one than at the age of sixty-one, but normal human beings can always go on learning. Education in this sense is not just the accumulation of facts, it is the acquisition of skills by which we can cope with the facts. To use my overworked computer analogy again: Education is the process by which the human computer is programmed to handle the data. Data storage—that is to say, the memorizing of facts—is entirely secondary.

Education is not something primarily associated with school or technical college or university; it takes place mainly in the home. Its really fundamental component is the habit of communication established in extreme infancy, within the first year of life before the child begins to talk at all. Here, at the very beginning, when the mother first starts to convert her animal baby into a human being, the sole purpose of education is to link things together, to establish communication, to make the child conscious that it is part of the family group. The separation of identity comes much later. But when it comes we British go over to the opposite extreme and carry self-identification much too far.

The fact that people in other countries do things quite differently need not mean that we are wrong, but the difference here is striking. In the less sophisticated corners of the world, the kind of isolated loneliness which we consider normal—the emphasis on the uniqueness of the individual self separated from all others—is never cultivated at all. The child is born into a community which consists of whole classes of fathers and mothers, brothers and sisters, uncles and aunts, cousins and so on. In almost any situation there are half a dozen or so individuals who can act as stand-ins for any other. Moreover this is not just a temporary phase of early childhood; most people spend their whole lives surrounded and supported by kinsfolk.

In such circumstances the normal mode of self-expression is to say: 'We do this', not 'I do this'.

Let me pursue this point: It is a very striking fact that almost everywhere outside the centres of western capitalism the normal emphasis of education is on group identity rather than individual identity. I believe that this is very relevant to our problem of fear.

We have all of us, at one time or another, experienced

the sense of personal relaxation combined with excitement which comes from close identification with a group. Giving a cheer to 'our side', whether it means supporting our school or our football team or even just occasionally our government, is enjoyable and exhilarating. It can also be dangerous. There is not much difference between a football crowd and a mob. What goes on here is complicated, and I don't think that anyone really claims to understand very much about the psychology of crowds, but one thing is quite clear: participation in a group reduces, for the time being, the individual's private feelings of personal anxiety. In contrast, every decision which I must make, by myself without the support of my fellows, intensifies anxiety.

Now our society provides a great variety of institutions into which the individual may merge his identity—family, school, sports club, trade union, church, firm, political party—there are literally dozens of contexts in which the lonely individual can sink his *I* into a collective *we* and gain greater confidence by doing so, yet paradoxically a great deal of our explicit educational effort, both at school and at home, is aimed in exactly the opposite direction.

The overt values of English formal schooling are that the individual should be self-reliant and show initiative. From the age of ten upwards the whole system becomes viciously competitive. The aim is to discover and cultivate the powers of latent leadership in the few with total disregard for the emotional suffering that this imposes on the many. In Britain this objective is common both to the private school system, which is rigged so as to preserve the vested interests of the wealthy, and to the State school system, which pretends to offer 'equal opportunity for all'.

In practice, the State system is devoted to the needs of a meritocracy in which all the rewards go to the most able.

In private sector and public sector alike, every attempt to introduce a touch of socialist justice—the principle 'from each according to his capacity: to each according to his needs'—is resisted up to the hilt. We are told that we must segregate the clever just as we must segregate the criminal; comprehensive schools, it is said, will 'lower educational standards' and ruin the nation! This isn't a straight issue of party politics—even among the Tories the really passionate opponents of comprehensive education stand well over to the right—but you have only to consider what happened in Enfield and then read some of the speeches made at the recent Conservative Party Conference to see how mixed up you can get. Many people take it for granted that the 'best' schools are those which cater for the children of the very rich. But if you can't afford to send your son to Eton then the next best thing is cut-throat competition—to the death.

This is a sad business. Even if it were true, which it isn't, that success at school and university guaranteed success in adult life, the rat race is conducted at terrible cost. Over the past fifty years we in England have partly replaced the old system of class stratification based on hereditary wealth by a new class system based on achieved status. Simultaneously our educational system has developed into an entirely ruthless machine for the elimination of the unworthy. Suicide and mental breakdown are now so common in student populations that they are almost taken for granted.

Let's try to get this straight. We instil competitive values into our children from entirely dishonest motives.

Few of us have any deep concern about whether our off-spring become civilized human beings; we are only worried about social class. We are hag-ridden by the fear and envy endemic to a society which combines class stratification with the possibility of social mobility. Those who are high up in the existing order are driven to compete by fear and contempt for those below; those lower down are driven by envy of those above. Schooling is a means to an end: the child must better himself, or consolidate an established position. Only a tiny minority thinks of education as a means by which individuals are given human interests and values so that they can fit together into the total jig-saw of society; for most of us education is an instrument of war, a weapon by which the individual beats down his competitors and defends himself against adversity. I assure you, I do not exaggerate.

It seems probable that everyone, including those who are now most successful, would feel much more comfortable in a less competitive world, and if we are looking towards the future this should be one of our long-term objectives. It won't be easy to achieve but this much is quite plain: In order to arrive at a system in which less value is placed on the relative merit of individuals we shall need to make quite basic changes to the overall structure of formal school education. If we are to produce adults who are inspired by an ethic of co-operation rather than an ethic of fratricide then we must start out by devising a school system in which passing competitive examinations and proving that Tom is much cleverer than Harry ceases to be part of the exercise.

Oh, I know this is very Utopian. A General Certificate of Education at A level is worth the money, and even more so a university degree. The child who finishes the hurdle race with a bit of paper which entitles him to write B.A. after his name has financially much better prospects than his brother who gets stuck at the 11+. This is why parents and children alike hurl themselves into the fray with such ferocity. If you take away the carrot of financial reward, standards really will fall all along the line. But this is only because the children and the parents and the schoolmasters and the university dons are all so totally confused.

The confusion starts out with a clash of basic assumptions. The schoolmasters and the dons tend to believe that innate intelligence is a quality which varies very greatly from one individual to another but that you can't do much about it except measure it. That being so, school education is not much concerned with 'developing the intelligence'; it simply stuffs the wretched pupil full of facts and measures the result by an examination. Parents, on the other hand, start out with the sentimental idea that the intellectual potential of all children is basically the same. In that case the only way to get your beloved child out in front is either to cheat by sending him to a privileged school, or to chastise and bully him so that he passes examinations which the other fellow fails.

Both sides are right up to a point; and both sides are entirely wrong. Intelligence is a very complicated affair involving a mixture of all sorts of mental capacities and psychological attitudes—powers of perception, memory, vocabulary, logical facility, curiosity, scepticism, persistence, the ability to make unexpected associations and goodness knows what else. The underlying mental faculties are inborn, the product of the individual's genetic constitution. No amount of education or parental devotion

68

will ever turn a dull boy into a genius. On the other hand, the way in which we use and develop our potential skills will be determined by things that happen to us *after* we are born. The trouble here is that many of the really critical events seem to occur very early on, perhaps even in the first few weeks of life or even in the course of the birth trauma itself, and I don't think that there is the slightest evidence that at this very early age a child is at an advantage if it happens to have a mother who is especially prosperous, or intelligent, or ambitious. Just how far the intellectual potential of a child can still be modified even after it reaches school age is a moot point; certainly the margin of flexibility is not very great. On the other hand, it is absolutely clear that by the time children do get to school they already have abilities of very different kinds. Also it is plain that any attempt to 'measure' intelligence by examination will simply measure certain sorts of ability and ignore the rest. But the open-ended non-measurable kind of ability may be just what we are looking for. I want to stress this.

In some ways the role of education in the development of the individual is much like the role of habitat in the natural selection of species. You may remember that much earlier on I made a distinction between species which have a very specialized adaptation to a very narrowly defined kind of environment, and versatile species which can survive in all sorts of conditions; the difference, say, between a rare alpine plant which can only exist at a particular altitude on the north face of a rock of a particular chemical composition, and a common garden weed. And I made the point that it is the versatile species, the weeds which are not tied down to any particular orthodoxy, which have the best prospect of survival in a rapidly changing world. Well, so it is with individuals. The people who are going to be able to cope with our rapidly changing future are those who are temperamentally unorthodox— the curious, the sceptical, the ones who don't care a fig for established opinion, people like Charles Darwin, who said of himself:

'I have steadily endeavoured to keep my mind free so as to give up any hypothesis, however much beloved, as soon as facts are shown to be opposed to it.'

Now if all this is true the implications for education should be fairly obvious. We should be looking for people with divergent unorthodox kinds of intelligence, not conformist orthodox types. But since all methods of selection by competitive examination can only be based on established orthodoxies, we must try to get rid of competitive examinations altogether. The aim must be to maximize variation. We need to give all children equal opportunity to learn how to learn, but after that they should be encouraged to follow their own special interests instead of the textbook conventions of examination syndicates.

Fine words, but what a hope! The academic machine is supposed to be searching for genius but, with things set up as they are now, it can only recognize those who are both very clever and very obedient. It turns out excellent bureaucrats but rejects or perhaps never notices those genuinely imaginative characters who refuse to toe the line.

Higher education is necessarily selective. It isn't everyone who can benefit from life in a university; but clearly those who do go to a university should include the innovators who are going to lead us forward into our bewildering future. To see what sort of people these are, we might consider who they have been in the past. Who are the people who really stand out over the past few centuries as having completely altered our Western view of where man stands in relation to the universe? Newton, Darwin, Marx, Freud, Picasso—there are only a dozen or so world shakers in this class. And if we ask: 'Are these the sort of people who are likely to flourish and gain approval in our present educational garden?' the answer in most cases must be an unqualified 'No'. Newton, it is true, was a life-long academic of extreme distinction, but even so in 1689 the Fellows of my College declared him to be an entirely unsuitable person to be their Provost[1]; the best that Cambridge could offer to Darwin was an ordinary degree; Marx, who lived in England for thirty-four years, was never noticed at all; and so on.

So to go right back to my original question: Yes, more and better education could help us to cope with the problems of an expanding technology, but only if we take a more enlightened view about what we mean by 'better' education. Education ought to be concerned with training people to exercise their imaginations creatively, instead of which it is too often little more than a selection device for picking out the clever conformists.

It wouldn't matter so much if educational diplomas simply gave a list of the courses in which the owner has shown reasonable proficiency; what is outrageous is that an entirely anonymous examination machine should have the arrogance to grade its victims as 'adequate', 'good',

---

[1] The Fellows might have overcome their prejudices but for the unfortunate fact that Newton's candidature was sponsored by the King. Cf. J. Saltmarsh, *King's College*, Cambridge, 1958, p. 63.

and 'excellent', without any personal knowledge and indeed without any evidence at all except a few written scripts compiled in a great hurry under highly artificial conditions. Let's face it, school and university examinations in their present form do not test ability or personality or knowledge, they simply test a capacity for passing examinations, an aptitude which is of rather marginal utility in ordinary adult life.

But the vested interest in examinations is very large, and certificates and class marks have enormous appeal to the bureaucratic mind, so it is difficult to get any anti-examination campaign off the ground. Competitive examinations give the appearance of objectivity and fairness. Those who operate more humane methods of selection are always suspected of favouritism and of rigging the market through private old-boy networks. But there is not much point in being fair to all if you still end up by picking out the wrong people.

In the context of my general theme, there are two main points I am getting at here. The first is the straightforward one that our competitive examination system of selection simply fails to pick out the kind of people who can cope most effectively with problems of social and technological change; the second is that the emphasis which our system places on individual achievement is entirely mis-directed.

Much of our adult state of fear is linked up with the feeling that I, an individual, have to cope single-handed with a hostile world, the details of which have become far too complicated for me to understand. This feeling of isolation is in part a by-product of the way we have been educated and the stress that is put on passing examinations.

The more 'successful' your education, the more likely you are to feel alone, because the process of segregation has been more complete. Just a few of you are academics like myself. 11+, O Level, A Level, College Entrance, Degree Class, Ph.D. . . . at every stage you proved how much cleverer you are than all those other fellows, until in the end you stand quite alone and afraid.

It ought to be possible to manage things in a different way so that we go forward into the future together, collaborating as a team instead of looking around for every possible opportunity to knife each other in the back.

Don't blame the schoolmasters for the kind of education you received; they crammed you with facts instead of teaching you how to enjoy the pleasures of civilization because the ethos of a competitive society compels them to behave in this way. If society insists that individuals be segregated out into categories—first class, second class, third class, upper, middle, lower—then the system will always have to waste an enormous amount of time and energy allocating individuals to the right slots and marking them up with the proper labels, but so far as education is concerned the whole operation is utterly irrelevant. Those of you who have, like me, been right through the mill know very well that this is so. It is up to us to get the system changed. Comprehensive schools are a beginning, but that is only the start.

But if examinations have nothing to do with education, what has? Education is concerned with the passing on of tradition, so we tend to think of the teacher as a wise old man, and a great deal of prestige still attaches to the teaching of history and ancient philosophy. This would be fair enough in a stable conservative society. Among the Australian Aborigines, for example, many crucial pieces of information about the environment—such as the location of waterholes, weather lore, and the habits of animals and plants—are treated as an esoteric form of knowledge known only to a small circle of very old men whose secrets are passed on bit by bit to the younger members of the tribe in the course of a long series of initiations.

But in societies like our own which are undergoing rapid development, it is the young adults, not the old ones, who possess the kind of knowledge which young people need to share before they can participate fully in what is going on. With us, for example, it is, by and large, the men under forty who 'know what is worth knowing'—the computer men, the microbiologists, the ethologists, the radio astronomers—in such fields anyone with a white hair in his head is already hopelessly out-of-date. Yet we still have the antiquated notion that education is a function in which the old teach the young. This point is terribly important. The pace of technological change is such that the opinions of the elderly become increasingly irrelevant. In our runaway world, no one much over the age of forty-five is really fit to teach anybody anything.[1] And that includes me. I am fifty-seven. It is hard to accept but that's just the point.

One major change that is needed in our society is that we should all recognize how quickly we are changing. It is

[1] Those who are 45 in 1968 were 16 at the outbreak of the Second World War. They had already left school before anyone had ever heard of computers, jet aircraft, nuclear fission, space rocketry, antibiotics . . .

quite essential that those in authority be persuaded to take a back seat much earlier on in their lives than they do at present. In the universities just now there is a good deal of talk about student power. The student body as a whole, or certain substantial chunks of it, is in an anarchist rebellious mood. It claims that the machinery of university education has become heartless and bureaucratic, that those who run the universities are taking far too little trouble to discover what the students themselves really want. As with all such complaints, facts get distorted and injustices exaggerated, but the students certainly have a case. University committees and university departments are all too often managed by old men—wise in experience but quite out of touch with what is now going on.

But this is not a peculiarity of universities. Professors are compulsorily retired at sixty-seven; much of British industry is directed (or misdirected) by elderly gentlemen well over seventy. Medical science is steadily increasing the expectation of life and this, combined with the concentration of industry into larger and larger units, is having the effect that an ever greater proportion of the final power of decision is being concentrated into the hands of very old men, which is the worst possible way of facing the problems of a rapidly changing future. Since those who hold offices of power will never willingly give them up, I believe that there is only one solution to this problem. The young must somehow or other enforce quite arbitrary rules of early retirement. In those parts of our system which are concerned with research and technological development, either in education, or in industry, or in politics, no one should be allowed to hold any kind of responsible administrative office once he has passed the age of fifty-five.[1]

In a changing world machines get obsolete very quickly; so do human beings. How can young people possibly have confidence in the advice and judgement of old men who freely admit that they are totally bewildered?

Certainly the young need to be educated; they need to be taught to gain confidence in the astonishing powers of their own imaginations. But they don't need to be loaded down with the out-of-date clutter of useless information which is all that traditional scholarship has to offer. Only those who hold the past in complete contempt are ever likely to see visions of the New Jerusalem.

The old are only competent to do the job that they were brought up to do—that is, to operate with the out-of-date over-simplified stereotypes that were current in their youth. Such people, and they include myself, are not qualified to plan a new world for the rising generation nor are they fit to train the young to cope with situations of which they themselves have had no experience. They can of course map out some of the difficulties and point up some of the more glaring deficiencies of the system as it is, which is roughly what I have been trying to do in these lectures. But the creation of a tolerable future is not a task which our present rulers could ever hope to undertake. Most of them should accept Voltaire's advice and retire gracefully to cultivate their own gardens.

---

[1] It has been interesting to observe how this suggestion that the elderly should be compelled to surrender their offices of *power* has, on all sides, been misconstrued as a proposal that all elderly persons should be made to abandon their ordinary occupations.

6 'Only connect . . .'

As an introductory text for these lectures I might very well have taken E. M. Forster's magic phrase: 'Only connect . . .'[1] All the way through I have been urging you to keep on remembering the total interconnectedness of things as distinct from their separate isolated existence. But there is more to it than that. In most cases the connectedness is dynamic, not static.

The starting point of any scientific inquiry is exact description, and description always leads us to break down big units into little ones and then stick neatly classified labels on to the component parts. But in complex systems we are inclined to oversimplify the pattern by which the parts are fitted together. A static complex, such as the interlocking arrangement of the gear wheels of a watch, is a much easier kind of model to hold in the mind than a dynamic complex, such as the organization of a machine in which all the component parts function in three dimensions and are made of elastic. Because of this, our education, which lays so much stress on tidy, over-elaborate classifications, makes us think that society ought to be organized like a watch rather than like a jellyfish. This bias produces conservative-minded people who take fright

[1] These words are printed beneath the title on the title page of *Howard's End*.

whenever they come up against the fluidity of real-life experience.

But there is also another reason why the traditional emphasis on classification has become inappropriate to contemporary education. It is becoming less and less important for the scientist to understand just what *are* the component parts of the natural world; the essential thing now is to know how the system works, how the bits fit together. If you give your son a radio kit for Christmas the bits and pieces are just so many black boxes. Unless he is a very unusual boy he does not understand in detail what these objects are; but he doesn't need to. Provided he follows the instructions carefully he can assemble the parts into a radio set and it will work.

Now I realize that the assembly of prefabricated machines is usually considered to be a very low grade kind of activity. At school the first introduction to science consists of taking something to pieces—dissecting a frog, for example; the much more creative operation of putting things together so that they work as a system is rated child's play, not learning.

I suggest that it is time that we turned these values back to front. 'Only connect . . .' It is not the bits and pieces that matter but the evolving system as a whole. And we are part of the system. I keep on repeating this, but it really isn't so easy. For centuries our whole education has been built up around the assumption that we rational human beings stand *outside* the system and that the human capacity for understanding the processes of nature by taking things apart has no limit. But it has. The runaway world is terrifying because we are gradually becoming aware that simple faith in the limitless powers of human rationality is an illusion. Quite ordinary unsophisticated people are beginning to be made aware of the implications of Gödel's Proof.

Sorry, that sounds like a piece of one-upmanship. I must explain what I am talking about. Kurt Gödel is a mathematician who, in 1931, demonstrated that there are limits to what can be shown to be true by mathematical logic. The implications of this are very complicated but one aspect of the matter is this: Gödel seems to show that because the human brain is an apparatus of a particular kind which is only capable of 'thinking' in a particular way, there are limits to what any particular individual can know to be certainly true.

Gödel also shows the importance of distinguishing within any field of our experience that part which is 'consistent' and which is on that account susceptible to completely rational analysis and that part which cannot be shown to be consistent and which therefore might contain elements of choice, uncertainty, imagination and so on.[1]

One inference from all this (which is relevant to what I have been saying) is that we shouldn't always expect the products of human imagination to fit tidily within the categories of thought which we possess already. We should expect the total framework of knowable truth to keep on evolving and expanding and changing shape along with the development and refinement of the categories which we use to describe it.

Let us consider how this affects my earlier proposition that 'men are machines and nothing more'. First we must

[1] See E. Nagel and J. R. Newman, *Gödel's Proof*, New York, 1958.

get away from the idea that the concept of 'machine' can only appropriately be used to describe artificial pieces of inorganic apparatus like motor cars and radio sets. The important thing about a machine is the way it works and what it does. And my point is that we can ask these questions: 'How does it work?' 'What does it do?' not only about things like motor cars and radio sets but also about organic processes and even about social institutions. But having said that, we must then understand that there is a difference between machines which are fully 'consistent' and machines which are not. For example, if I have a mechanical calculator and I instruct it to add together two and two, then the form of its response is exactly predictable, the apparatus behaves consistently. If however I ask *you* to write on a piece of paper the sum of two plus two, I can't predict what you will do—not even if I am quite sure that you know the right answer and that you are willing to co-operate, for some of you may write the word 'four' in capitals and some in small letters, or if you were to write the answer in figures you could do it in all sorts of different ways. But the striking thing is that this variation in behaviour on your part would make no real difference: you would still all be giving the right answer.

The general point is this: It is a peculiar feature of the human communication system that if an individual A wants to say something to another individual B, he can convey his message through an indefinitely large number of alternative channels. Yet, provided A and B both share the same cultural background, B will always understand what is being said. That is a very astonishing kind of circus trick which no man-made machine could as yet come anywhere near to achieving. You may be a machine of a sort but you are not just a piece of clockwork.

This human flexibility, which permits us to respond to external stimuli in a variety of different ways, should be very reassuring. We are not completely bound by what has happened before. It is natural to man, just as it is natural to any other animal species, to order his environment by fitting it into the categories of his expectations. We thus come to attach emotional value to the descriptive words by which our parents and our schoolmasters have explained the circumstances of existence. As more and more data accumulate we try to fit it all into the simplified slots which early education provided; when we fail to do this, panic ensues; the world seems to be running away, we are rushing headlong to chaos. The jobs we have to do just won't fit any more with the official regulations and the Trade Union rule book. But you don't have to rely on the old-established categories; you can invent new ones. Your reserves of intellectual capacity are very great, and if things seem chaotic this can only be because you have never seriously tried to make use of your potential ability to cope with the unexpected. Believe it or not, every one of you is quite astoundingly inventive and resourceful. Your linguistic behaviour demonstrates this quite clearly. When you are chatting to a neighbour on a bus or gossiping over a cup of tea a great many of the things you say are simply repetitive phrases which you have uttered many times before, but every time you engage in serious argument you can spontaneously invent huge chunks of brand new sound pattern which no one in the course of human history has ever heard before, yet you and your listening audience can both immediately understand what is being said. Creatures with god-like powers of this sort have no need to be afraid of the complexity of changing situations.

I am not asking you to be smug. There are factors in the situation around us which scare me out of my wits, but it isn't change that fills me with dread. Just the opposite. What is really alarming is our immense reluctance to alter our expectations. Take weaponry for example. The monstrous arsenal of modern armaments is manipulated by politicians who talk as if the concept of national sovereignty had remained completely unchanged ever since the eighteenth century. Generals who can fire rockets to the moon conduct their debates as if everyone were armed with bows and arrows. The real danger here is not the sophistication of the technology, it is the antediluvian mentality of the military advisers, and of those whom they advise. These prehistoric attitudes have their repercussions right across society and in particular they demoralize the young. For example:

One of the more surprising features of the contemporary scene is that, despite lavish financial prospects, large numbers of exceptionally able young people resolutely decline to pursue an orthodox scientific career. Candidates for university social science courses are turned away in their hundreds, while vacancies in the traditional natural sciences go begging. The phenomenon is quite recent, and it may be temporary, but it isn't peculiar to Britain; it has been reported from all over Western Europe and from the United States. All sorts of explanations have been suggested. Some are just silly, such as that schoolboys think social science is easy and that they would rather not go to university at all if it means doing some hard work; other explanations seem more plausible, such as the argument that the great demand for trained scientists since the war has meant a decline in the quality of science teaching in schools, so schoolboys get the idea that pure science is dull. But quite a lot of the trouble seems to result from straight emotional distress. The young are just appalled at the way that science is being used: Hiroshima, Vietnam, Dr Kahn's calculations of mega-death. And even when the experts give over planning the total destruction of humanity, they contemplate quite casually the destruction of nature itself. 'Let's build an airfield at Aldabra. It will only cost about twenty million pounds, two or three rare species of animal, and the lives of several million birds. No one has ever heard of the damned place anyway.'

Aldabra, in case you don't know, is a small island in the Indian Ocean, the principal home of the frigate bird and the giant tortoise and one of the few natural zoological laboratories still remaining anywhere on earth. Up until a few weeks ago, despite the most vigorous protests by the whole scientific community, the British Government had planned to destroy the place just to provide a temporary staging post for the RAF. It is only the sterling crisis and the reluctance of the United States to join in which has at last persuaded the authorities that this is an extravagance we cannot afford. So devaluation has at least prevented you from aiding and abetting an international crime! What horrifies is not that Air Marshals should contemplate such things but that the whole administrative machine of our country, including ministers in the Cabinet, should operate with a system of values which makes such action seem morally respectable. It is the bland unquestioned assumption that national interests always override human interests and that what is man-made and artificial always has priority over what is wild and natural. For me such attitudes are criminal—criminal in just the same sense as Hiroshima was criminal and Hitler's attempt to exterminate the Jews was criminal. The scale is different but the offence is of the same kind. It is the monstrous misuse of man's newly discovered supernatural power. Actions of this sort can only occur when the decision-maker is totally disorientated about the relations which link ourselves to other people and mankind to nature. But it is men who are blameworthy, not science. Science in itself is neutral; it is neither cohesive nor disruptive. In the hands of men of goodwill it intensifies understanding and connectedness; in the hands of the sick it is an instrument of violence and alienation. The young observe the sickness of their elders and they refuse to be corrupted. But this is a grave matter, for the future certainly lies with the men of science and it is altogether essential that they should be men of imagination and men of goodwill. The last thing that we can afford is to abandon the laboratories to military maniacs and politicians.

What then is to be done about it? My purpose in these talks has not been to preach a sermon but to try to show you how things are—that is to say, how *you* are in relation to the rest. Of course, there are lots of aspects of the world around us which are, on the face of it, 'in a runaway condition': population growth, technological growth, the destruction of nature, to name only three. The popular delusion is that such issues constitute problems which can be solved by pursuing the right policy. What I have been saying is that there cannot be any *right* policy in the traditional sense because any policy to which values like 'good' or 'bad' could possibly be attached would simply represent the advantage of some particular group of people; the whites as against the non-whites, the haves as against the have-nots, the old as against the young. But you will find no respite to your anxieties by trying to opt out. The 'it's none of my affair, let them get on with it' attitude will, in the long run, only make you more panic-stricken than before. What is needed is that you should come to see where you fit in. The more that each one of us can come to understand the overall inter-connectedness of things, the more likely it is that we shall collectively generate an attitude which will not result in self-destruction. What is important is not that you should know what to do, but that you should feel really deeply that all parts of the system are of equal importance.

Let us go back to the beginning. All animals cope with existence by fitting their experience into categories which they expect. This essentially is what we mean when we say that, by the process of evolution, animals become adapted to specialized environments. If the experience cannot be fitted into the expectations, then the animal cannot behave in an appropriate manner and it fails to survive. Human beings, like all other animals, are thus very strongly motivated to try to fit new experiences into old categories—to make it seem as if what was happening corresponded to our expectations. In this respect our human ability to form verbal concepts and share them with others provides us with enormous flexibility, and this seems to be the principal factor which has worked to our adaptive advantage in competition with other animal species. Human beings are superior to other animals because they have wider choice in the way they can slot experience into expectation, and because they have developed a greater variety of systems of communication. It is our capacity to communicate rather than our capacity to interbreed which has in the past saved the species from disintegration into a number of specialized sub-types, and if we are to maintain our human cohesion and human dominance it is essential that we allow these two advantages to go on evolving. We must act positively so as to inhibit the tendency for individuals and groups of individuals to separate out as specialized non-communicating systems, and we must stimulate the young to elaborate and enlarge their expectations in imaginative ways so that even the most bizarre new experience can be treated as plausible, and therefore subject to control.

These are simple phrases, but they have deep implications. They imply that every manifestation of national consciousness is an evil; that respect for tradition is an evil; that every vested interest is at all times open to challenge. They imply a political philosophy of continuous revolution, a persistent disrespect for all forms of bureaucracy. And of course very few of you could possibly accept such a doctrine. But there you have your choice. You can go on believing that the world ought to be an orderly place even though the quite obvious absence of order fills you with terror, or you can revel in the anarchy and thereby recover your faith in the future instead of hankering after a long dead past.

Most of us are far too deeply embedded in our conventional orthodoxies to embark on such an adventure, but at least we have a duty to show the next generation where they might choose to go. It is the underlying attitudes implicit in our educational system that need to be changed.

European learning over the past two thousand years has rested on the assumption that all the essential categories of thought had already been devised by the fifth century BC. The art of civilized living has consisted of slotting all new experiences into Ancient Greek categories—and then we knew how to cope. This expedient has worked surprisingly well for a surprisingly long time, but it has now completely broken down. We must face up to this. Education must show quite explicitly at every level that the battery of concepts borrowed from Plato and Aristotle and the Bible, which served so well in the past, is not adequate for the twentieth century. If the old want to regain the confidence of the young then the first thing they must do is to give up the pretence that they know everything already.

Education should also pay much closer attention to the way our attitudes are controlled by language. The young are taught to think that they are permanently engaged in a military campaign—they must 'triumph' over their adversities, they must 'conquer' outer space, they must 'gain victory' over disease, they must 'defeat' international communism, but this is the language of fear—of petty minded people who suspect in their hearts that they are going to be overwhelmed. What is needed is greater confidence. Young people need to be shown that they are already in a position of supremacy; their problem is not to conquer the environment, but to look after it.

And we must get out of the habit—which arises from the way our schools are organized—of thinking that reason and imagination are two different kinds of 'thing', that the truth of mathematics relates to one kind of fact and the truth of poetry to something quite different. We are all together in one world and what we are conscious of is one experience.

The unique and astonishing thing about human beings is not simply their capacity to observe and analyse the contents of the world around them, but their capacity to create. Every one of us is an artist with words. We create brand new sentences, we don't just imitate old ones. And, as you speak, you generate consciousness; what you create is yourself. That is a god-like activity.

It is time that we had done with the idea that humility is a virtue. As long as we are taught to be humble we shall go on using our imaginations to create enemies on every side: communists, vermin, bacteria, viruses, flying saucers —and we shall go on feeling that we shall only be safe if we sterilize our surroundings with bombs and chemicals and lethal disinfectants. What the young have got to learn is that they are masters of the situation; they can afford to come to terms with their surroundings, rather than obliterate them.

This is a lesson we have had to learn many times before. Ever since human language first created a world full of separate species, human beings have been trying to understand just where they fit in. Are the wild animals our friends or our enemies, our neighbours or our relatives, our masters or our servants? Today's monsters are of a different kind—strange political systems, new diseases, new drugs, machines which think—but the old problems remain. Are the 'others' enemies or friends, servants or masters?

Well, what did we do about it in the beginning?

We do not know much about how our first ancestors lived, how they talked, or how they owed respect to leaders, whether they had organized families or whether they killed one another; but there are one or two rather odd and surprising things. We know for certain that even thirty thousand years ago there were artists in the south of France who could paint bulls and horses with the assured mastery of a Picasso and we know—or at least we think we know—that long long before that men began to cook their food instead of eating it raw.

Now it isn't a biological necessity that you should cook your food, it is a custom, a symbolic act, a piece of magic which transforms the substance and removes the contamination of 'otherness'. Raw food is dirty and dangerous; cooked food is clean and safe. So already, even at the very beginning, man somehow saw himself as 'other' than nature. The cooking of food is both an assertion of this otherness and a means of getting rid of the anxiety which otherness generates.

But what about that stone-age Picasso? Just what the prehistoric artists of Lascaux thought they were up to when they painted their bulls and their cows and their horses and their swimming deer is anybody's guess, but here too it is a case of taming the other. The pictures show large and dangerous wild animals, not men. To make a painting of an animal is to transform it—the painted animal is like cooked food; it may be powerful but it has ceased to be dangerous, it has been brought under control. And it surely deserves remark that although, with rare exceptions, all the animals depicted in the ancient cave paintings of Southern France and Spain have their modern farm-yard descendants, these species were tamed by the magic ritual of paint many many thousands of years before they were tamed by domestication!

Art and poetry are the power to transform, the ability to take nature to pieces and recreate it; it is dangerous but it is magical and it has been man's heritage from the beginning. The moral of my prehistoric parable is that if you really want to find a way out of our modern dilemma, you should talk with artists and poets rather than with university dons. But let me repeat once more: Divine inventiveness is latent in us all—in you and in me—it is not reserved for genius. But do not forget that it is the power of destruction as well as the power of creation. By all means let's make the most of our powers and enjoy our struggles with confusion, but at the same time, whenever we assert dominance over the universe, let's remember how things are connected up. The good and the bad, the weak and the strong, all have a right to exist. When next you spray those beans with insecticide, just pause to think how impoverished the world will be when the hawks and the owls and the butterflies have entirely disappeared, which won't be very long either. And likewise when your good liberal conscience next leads you to support some political crusade for the rights of national minorities, bear in mind that the other side of *that* penny is the fragmentation of the world, the violence between black and white, Pakistani and Indian, Sinhalese and Tamil, Turk and Cypriot, Jew and Arab. It is nationalism, not technology, which is our contemporary disaster, the lamentable delusion that only the separate can be free.

And that is the sum of what I have been saying. We can never be separate. We live in an evolving society as part of nature. In nature species do not evolve in isolation but in combination. The species which survive are the 'fittest', but fitness to survive is a very complicated matter. It is not

just the equivalent of ruthless efficiency and aggression—
'nature red in tooth and claw' and all that stuff. A species
which is so efficient that it eliminates all its competitors is
likely to find that it has destroyed its own food supply. To
be fit to survive you must be content to share your living
space with other living things. You can be as free as you
choose; but only if you choose not to carry freedom to
excess. If we choose always to ignore the interests of our
neighbours, whether they be human or sub-human, we
shall, in the last chapter, simply be dead.

'Live and let live' is not an heroic creed and, as a
panacea for a world out of control, it hardly seems
adequate to the circumstances, but the problems ahead
are too big for heroic solutions. It is attitudes, not actions,
which matter now; and certainly if all men believed in
tolerance we should not need to fear the bomb.

But tolerance is not such a negative creed either. Right
at the beginning of these talks I said that we must recognize that we are now responsible for the future. We
cannot 'leave it to Fate'. But that does not mean that we
must plan the future in detail; the most that we should
try to do is to determine the general direction in which
things move. We cannot inhibit the curiosity of the
scientists; they will explore the secrets of the universe as
they choose. But we can determine, in a general sense,
how the knowledge of the scientists is exploited so that it
affects the lives of the rest of us. If we had all been educated
so that values of toleration instead of values of aggressive
competition were uppermost in our minds, we would take
it for granted that long-term problems of nature conserv-
ancy were much more important than short-term problems
of air defence, we would recognize at once the absurdity

of building aircraft carriers and the utter barbarity of flogging schoolboys. Since we were not educated that way we are still frightened and vindictive but at least we can ensure that those who come after us are a little more civilized than ourselves.

But if tolerance is too difficult let us at any rate be optimistic and self-confident. If the prospect of a runaway world fills you only with dread rather than excitement, if your private prognosis of the next fifty years includes mass murder, mass starvation and the dictatorship of a name-less machine, then I can only beg you to take courage:

'Men at some time are masters of their fates.'

We *could* act like gods. That does not mean that we can control the universe but that we can act confidently with a sense of purpose. I have said it before. Gods are no more likely to achieve their private ambitions than are mere men who suffer the slings and arrows of outrageous fortune, but gods have much more fun.

Postscript

The Reith Lectures for 1967 had a *succès de scandale*. Broadly speaking, commentators were of three kinds. First there were the professional experts in broadcasting technique, both inside and outside the BBC, who were interested not so much in what was said as in the manner of my saying it. Here there seemed to be fairly general agreement that the style, both of language and of delivery, was well suited to the purpose on hand. But it may be worth reminding the reader of this book that the spoken word communicates its message in a different way from the written word and that a satisfactory broadcast talk is not necessarily a satisfactory written essay, or *vice versa*.

The second set of commentators were the journalists and journalist-academics who published criticisms for a fee. Here the tone was fairly consistently hostile, in some cases quite virulently so. Grounds for complaint varied but included three recurrent themes: it was said that my argument was confused, the analysis superficial, and the conclusions banal. The most striking example of this style of attack was provided by a plainly very agitated, though anonymous, intellectual who took up four pages of the magazine *Encounter* to denounce the whole enterprise as an 'intellectual disaster'. In all these cases the lack of communication was total and reciprocal. I can no more understand my critics than they can understand me and the only comment I can offer is the obvious one: If these lectures are so trivial, why give them such an inordinate amount of gratuitous publicity?

The third main body of comment came from members of the general public who had listened to or read the lectures of their own free choice. Here the response was quite different. Most of the reactions were positive and cordial, and I was repeatedly praised for my lucidity which was said to be 'so different from the usual academic talks on the Third Programme'. I received altogether over 500 individual letters and, in a great many cases, it was quite evident that the writer had fully understood what I was saying, quite irrespective of whether or not he or she agreed with my position.

Who then should judge the absolute merits of the case? I am naturally predisposed to think that my opponents have been somewhat unfairly biassed. I suspect that every journalist-academic is a Reith Lecturer *manqué*. He too longs in his heart for an opportunity to address a mass audience on a theme of his own choosing; yet for an academic to step down from his pedestal and actually talk about academic problems in plain unprofessional ordinary language is a kind of treachery; it almost suggests that the isolated pedantry of ordinary academic life is a fraudulent activity. The obvious reprisal is to denounce the traitor as a 'false intellectual' and that is precisely the position that most of my more hostile critics have managed to adopt.

But perhaps the heart of the matter lies elsewhere. Professor Alasdair MacIntyre has made the interesting ob-servation that if Reith Lectures are to be 'successful', in the sense that they catch the attention of the mass audience to whom they arc addressed, they must necessarily belong to the genre of sermons, but that journalist-academics are not used to listening to sermons! My critics judged my performance either as a bad political speech or a bad university lecture; the more amateur commentators had fewer preconceptions and simply listened to what I had to say.

The difficulty about the Reith Lectures from the lecturer's point of view lies in the nature of his audience. It is extremely large and includes individuals of an immense variety of backgrounds and levels of education. Although some people listen to the whole series of lectures from start to finish the majority of each week's audience is starting out from scratch. Consequently the link between the individual lectures has to be a persistent thread rather than an expanding river. The lecturer cannot 'go back to what we were saying last week' and start piling on the detail. Most of those who are listening did not hear 'what we were saying last week'. That being so, the style of delivery is bound to be asseverative; the lecturer can only assert what he believes to be the case, there is no possibility that he should be able to marshal the evidence which might help to show that his assertions are true. This put me at a disadvantage whenever I was expressing opinions which my critics did not wish to accept. A case in point is my dogmatic assertion that all moral values are arbitrary (p. 48) which was countered by Mr Philip Toynbee's equally dogmatic assertion (*The Observer*, 7 January 1968, page 13) that 'moral fundamentals remain remarkably unchanged'. The fact that I could have cited whole libraries of ethnographic evidence in support of my contention whereas Toynbee's view must rest on faith alone is not likely to impress the ordinary reader of this book. In the circumstances there seems little point in trying to provide chapter and verse for everything that I have said. I can only assure the reader that, apart from the retraction covered by the footnote on p. 32, I believe all the *factual* statements in these lectures are verifiable and accurate. In addition, of course, I have advanced a number of arguments which are matters of opinion rather than of fact—the relational view of consciousness (pp. 29, 30) for example, or my psychological assumption that an individual who adopts 'detached' attitudes in one sphere of activity will be predisposed to adopt detached attitudes in others. But I do not feel that I am called upon to apologize for such opinions. The Reith Lecturer is provided with a unique opportunity to expound his personal beliefs to a mass audience. What I have said in these lectures is what I believe to be the case.

But the passages which aroused the greatest controversy were neither statements about readily verifiable facts nor simple expressions of opinion, but propositions about the use of words. The hostility of my critics was triggered off by my refusal to accept the conventional wisdom which is embodied in stereotyped verbal formulae about the 'holiness' of family life, the 'permissiveness' of contemporary society, the 'respect' due to the elderly and to established institutions, and so on. Consider, for example, the case of 'the permissive society'. One of the recurrent themes throughout my lectures is that our social system is exceptionally intolerant of abnormality. This thesis appeared to madden my critics, who kept on making blind assertions to the contrary, saying that our permissiveness is self-evident—and, by implication, regrettable. How should such an issue be settled? From my point of view there is really nothing to argue about. We can *measure* the degree of permissiveness in any society by considering what areas of daily life are intended to be controlled by formal regulation, by noting the variety of closed institutions—prisons, reform schools, mental hospitals, etc.—which are made available for the segregation of the abnormal, and by assessing the efficiency of the social machinery by which particular individuals are sorted out and incarcerated in such institutions. By *all* such criteria Britain in 1968 has a quite exceptionally intolerant social system. To assert otherwise seems to me just silly.

And so also with many other matters over which I was taken to task. Perhaps it was a little unfair to refer to the stranglehold of H.P. indebtedness in a competitive society as the 'tawdry secrets' of the family without explaining just what I meant (p. 44)—my critics seemed to assume that I must be talking about sexual scandals and that I had got my language wrong! I have to admit that at times I trailed my coat just to get a reaction, but I still meant what I said, and the actual reaction often astonished me. I would myself have supposed that all references to the family which appear in Lecture 3 are entirely commonplace, yet on this subject the critics came after me as if my whole argument was a series of obscene blasphemies.

Against this emotional background any attempt to offer a point by point reply to my commentators would be a waste of effort. So let me only repeat that I believe in what I have said. Of course, lots of other people believe in these things too. It has all been said many times before even if not quite in this style. What I had to say was banal just as the content of any Christian sermon is banal. But that really is part of the trouble.

Conventional Christian listeners found themselves in agreement with much of what I was saying, so they concluded that in those other, less congenial, less familiar parts of the argument I must be muddled and confused. That I believe is an incorrect assessment. If the argument of this book has any merit it is precisely that it is all of a piece. Those who cannot recognize this unity have failed to understand what I am trying to say. Evolutionary humanism is a total attitude to the human situation; it is not just a nice job lot of Christian-sounding moral precepts. The essence of my argument is the total interconnectedness of things and ideas and it is because they cannot really face up to the implications of this interconnectedness that my critics find parts of my thesis so objectionable.